DEATH RAP
TUPAC SHAKUR : A LIFE

BARNABY LEGG   JIM McCARTHY   FLAMEBOY

OMNIBUS PRESS

LONDON / NEW YORK / PARIS / SYDNEY / COPENHAGEN / BERLIN / MADRID / TOKYO

Cover designed by Flameboy & Barnaby Legg
Book designed by Flameboy
Text by Barnaby Legg & Jim McCarthy

ISBN: 1.84449.727.5
Order Number: OP50633

Exclusive Distributors
Music Sales Limited,
8/9 Frith Street, London W1D 3JB, UK.

Music Sales Corporation,
257 Park Avenue South, New York, NY 10010, USA.

Macmillan Distribution Services,
53 Park West Drive, Derrimut, Vic 3030, Australia.

To the Music Trade only:
Music Sales Limited,
8/9 Frith Street, London W1D 3JB, UK.

Printed by: Kyodo, Singapore.

Special thanks to Kevin Hopgood for his inking services on pages 61 to 79.

A catalogue record for this book is available from the British Library.

Visit Omnibus Press on the web at www.omnibuspress.com

TUPAC SHAKUR
INTRODUCTION

By Nick Hasted

The hideous, half-seen figure of Jim Crow that haunts this graphic novel gives appropriate context to the short life of Tupac Shakur. His shooting on September 7, 1996 (he died six days later), and the conspiracy theories that have since swirled around it, make him, for many, one more victim of racism's curse on America. That is the epic history *Tupac: Death Rap* places him in, boldly interweaving the murders of Malcolm X and Marvin Gaye, the beating of Rodney King and the apocalypse of the 1992 LA riot, a tapestry of black American destruction shown to have its seeds in slavery and its brutal aftermath. As Jim Crow's final appearance as the bestial owner of a cracked country guitar suggests, Tupac's story is a blues as old as America.

But *Death Rap* also keeps sight of Tupac's contradictions as a human being, the fatal flaws that made him hurry to his own downfall. The comics' visual strengths daringly bring him back to life, and re-imagine what that life meant.

Tupac wore the mantle of a martyr almost from birth in 1971, to ex-Black Panther Afeni Shakur. He was never sure who his father was, but knew the most likely candidate had died of a crack overdose. Afeni called him her Black Prince, but raised him in the harsh realities of the poor. Her own eventual crack addiction and itinerant journeys across America, as she tried to find a safe harbour for her and her son, left him feeling like an outsider everywhere. "My major thing growing up was I couldn't fit in," he would recall. Still his mother, with her revolutionary dreams kept from the Sixties, made him feel destined for more. The teenage Tupac was a vulnerable artistic loner with a soft, feminine face, adding to the fatherless boy's feelings of unmanly weakness. He may have been at his happiest when he was 15, studying Shakespeare and ballet in Baltimore. But when Afeni sent him to California in 1988, that only made him feel more alienated. "I dressed like a hippie," he remembered later. "I couldn't play basketball. I thought I was weird because I was writing poetry, and I hated myself. I used to keep it a secret… I was really a nerd."

This was the sensitive, educated boy that would surface in later moments of happiness, the committed artist many of the film directors who worked with Tupac remembered with affection. He was so nearly the opposite of the doomed, violent black cliché he would die as. But American culture offered few places for nerdy, nice young black men, the brutal streets of California's ghettos still less. Regularly beaten by gangs for his soft, strange appearance, he followed the classic path of the bullied, and assumed a mask of macho numbness himself. He let his first, defining film role, as Bishop in Ernest Dickerson's *Juice* (1992, the same year as his debut LP, *2pacalypse Now*), leak into his life. Bishop was a cold yet manic teenage killer, idolising movie gangsters Jimmy Cagney and Al Pacino, unable to differentiate between their cackling fantasies and real life as he gunned down friends and foes, before being shot himself. The film's violence gave Tupac an aura of charismatic menace he had never managed on the real streets, which he was by now scouring for rap material. A man with no fixed centre, he embraced his new image, blurring celluloid and reality as badly as Bishop. He publicly sided with real LA gangstas the Bloods in their feud with the Crips, then at its terrifying zenith. Where LA's first gangsta-rappers, N.W.A., had associated themselves with the gangs as a marketing opportunity, Tupac, never really a hard man, had to go further.

The unhinged rage Jim McCarthy, Barnaby Legg and Flameboy show in his eyes as he beats a man on the night of his own murder suggests the brutal descent he now began. The struggle between his old sensitive Jekyll on delicate, feminist tracks like 'Brenda Got A Baby' and the lazy, violence-venerating Hyde of the more typical 'Thug Life' made his work fascinating. Half-hearted attempts to put gangstaism behind him, after his latest beating, shooting or jailing, marked out his real life. But too often, fantasies of martyrdom ruled his mind. "All the good niggas," he once declared, "all the niggas who change the world die in violence." His mother's cot-side crooning to her Black Prince was in those words. But so too was the seemingly inescapable strain of death and disgrace in black American public life.

Michael Jackson, O.J. Simpson and Mike Tyson - who Tupac watched fight on the night of his fatal shooting, feeling kinship - are among the latest black giants to be brought low. From Martin Luther King and Malcolm X to James Brown, Chuck Berry and Sly Stone, sex, drugs and violence seem to hunt down every example of black success. The stories of those who largely escaped this cycle, such as Curtis Mayfield or Jay-Z, never seem to loom quite so large. *Death Rap* demonstrates the seemingly random yet pervasive nature of this curse, pasting the Number of the Beast on Marvin Gaye's head as his vicious preacher father shoots him down, and watching a black assassin do the same to Malcolm X. But Jim Crow flies over more anonymous black bodies, too. This comic's most disturbing scene shows the random drive-by shooting of a young black boy on a sunny LA street, the bullet searing through his ribcage, on its way to destroying his lungs. When Tupac is shot later by unknown assailants at a New York recording studio, it is part of this wider pattern, just as the trials of Jackson and Simpson hint at the massively disproportionate jailing of young black men in America (and removal of male role models from their children, so repeating the cycle). That is why so many black Americans cheered the release of Simpson, seeing not a millionaire buying the best defence, but one more persecuted brother. This sense of a racist conspiracy lying in wait for black America's best and brightest is also central to Tupac's posthumous appeal, where he's seen as a sainted street martyr.

It was an image he had assiduously cultivated while he was alive. *Makaveli* (1996), the album that entered the charts after his death, showed Tupac crucified on its sleeve, a true rap messiah. On one level, he was continuing the grandiose sense of persecution of his previous two albums, *All Eyes On Me* (1996) and *Me Against The World* (1995). Prodigious dope intake and a general sense of justified paranoia in West Coast rap culture after the

King beating and LA riot was exaggerated for Tupac by regular criminal conviction, culminating in jail-time in 1995 for his part in the gang-rape of Ayanna Jackson.

Makaveli's cover also played into rap's sentimental fatalism, as his fatally linked rival Biggie Smalls (aka The Notorious B.I.G.) did on *Ready To Die* (1994) and *Life After Death* (1997), the latter informed by Tupac's murder but released days after Biggie's own, an event so seemingly predestined it hardly counted as irony. Tupac's 'How Long Will They Mourn Me?' (1994) had also played with death, like the assault rifle tattooed on his stomach. But his attempted murder in that New York studio lobby in 1995, when he was shot five times in the head and groin, losing a testicle, made his end suddenly seem all too real, and his survival a miracle. McCarthy and Flameboy catch this messianic moment perfectly, as they show the sad-eyed Tupac raising himself from the linoleum where he's been left for dead, his bloody bullet-holes like stigmata, his bandanna a crown of thorns. When he reaches the eighth-floor studio where Biggie has been working with his Bad Boy label boss Sean Combs (aka "Puff" Daddy), he's stared at like a ghost.

His legend was increased when, mummified in bandages outside the hospital, he gave reporters the finger. Checking himself out almost immediately, he attended his rape trial. When his wounds healed, that saw him jailed for sexual abuse and forced fondling. He'd certainly come a long way since ballet classes in Baltimore, but his credibility now hit a perverse high. Like 50 Cent's multiple bullet-scars today, there's nothing more "real" in rap than getting shot to pieces for no good reason. Tupac certainly crowed about his invincibility, after beating the odds once. But he also jumped when cars back-fired, and had terrible headaches where a bullet had passed near his skull. In this sense, his life had become as real as that of any of his fans still trapped back on ghetto streets, even as he also seemed larger than life, a resurrected, unrepentant gangsta.

The finishing touch to this brutal myth, Tupac surely knew, would only come when he truly died in a hail of bullets. The sense that, like Jesus, or many ghetto kids, he only had a short time on this earth, must explain the 19-hour days he spent in the studio rapping with obsessive intensity. He was providing the ammunition for his own musical after-life. At the last count, he has released seven albums since his death, more than when he was breathing. It has made him an ectoplasmic, seemingly immortal presence in the charts.

But Tupac's existence today as black saint, victim, martyr and myth does not go unchallenged by *Death Rap*. He was at least in the room when Ayanna Jackson was gang-raped, and went to jail by right. He attacked *Menace II Society* directors the Hughes Brothers with hip-hop's usual mob-handed thuggery, and gleefully joined in beating Orlando Anderson on the night of his own fatal shooting. His raps bragged of violence and taunted perceived enemies right to the end, even as, on convicted criminal Marion "Suge"

Knight's Death Row Records, he worked with the Bloods and Crips Knight kept on staff, the gap between art and actual consequences rarely in pop history more perilously thin. His extremely promising movie career and ability to rap far beyond gangsta clichés meant he had a way out. He was too weak to take it.

Tupac's feud with Biggie, "Puff" Daddy, Bad Boy and the whole of East Coast rap, stoked by Death Row's gangsta-minded West Coasters, and made personal by his probably unfounded suspicion of their involvement in his first shooting, made Tupac's murder in Vegas in September 1996, like Biggie's six months later, seem like the result of rap's penchant for "battles" reaching absurd extremes.

Wilder conspiracy theories soon inevitably grew around the bloodshed. But almost alone among pop deaths, in Tupac's case the conspiracy was real. Nick Broomfield's film *Biggie And Tupac* (2002) and the books *Have Gun Will Travel* (1998) by Ronin Ro and *LAbyrinth* (2002) by Randall Sullivan were among the unusually authoritative investigations spun from the deaths of the two rappers. They pointed to a final twist in the web of racial hurt, artistic hubris and personal confusion that characterised Tupac's life. He had, it turned out, been considering leaving Death Row, and wanted many millions in unpaid royalties. "Suge" Knight, with a reputation for brutality unmatched in music business history, and employees including LA gangstas and a Mob-linked lawyer, was not a man to cross. *Biggie And Tupac* and the heavily-documented *LAbyrinth* both place the occupants of the white Cadillac that sprayed Tupac with bullets then sped away as corrupt black LAPD members, moonlighting for Death Row. A black conspiracy, it seems, killed and completed a black icon.

Tupac: Death Rap stays with a broader picture: of Tupac as a case study in America's centuries-old capacity for racism and violence, and the way pop music can hold a mirror to it. It puts vividly fresh flesh on a familiar anti-hero, ignoring cautious biography for the more fundamentally truthful imaginative leaps of comic-book myth.

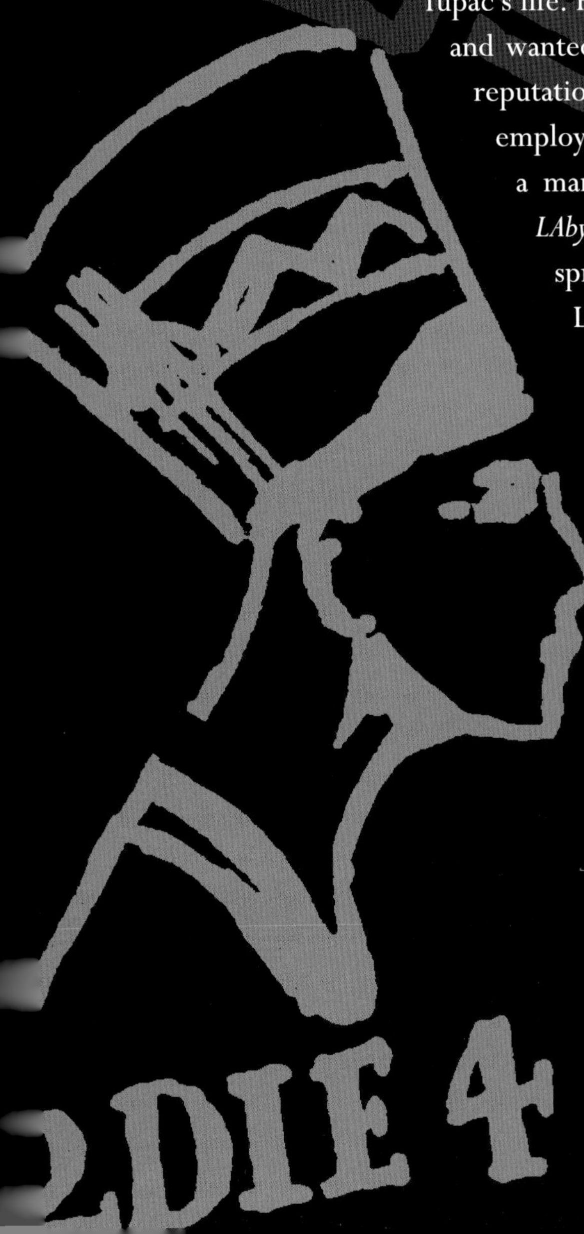
DIE 4

Nick Hasted is the author of The Dark Story of Eminem *(Omnibus Press, 2003). He writes on music, movies, books and comics for* The Independent, The Guardian, *and* Uncut *magazine.*

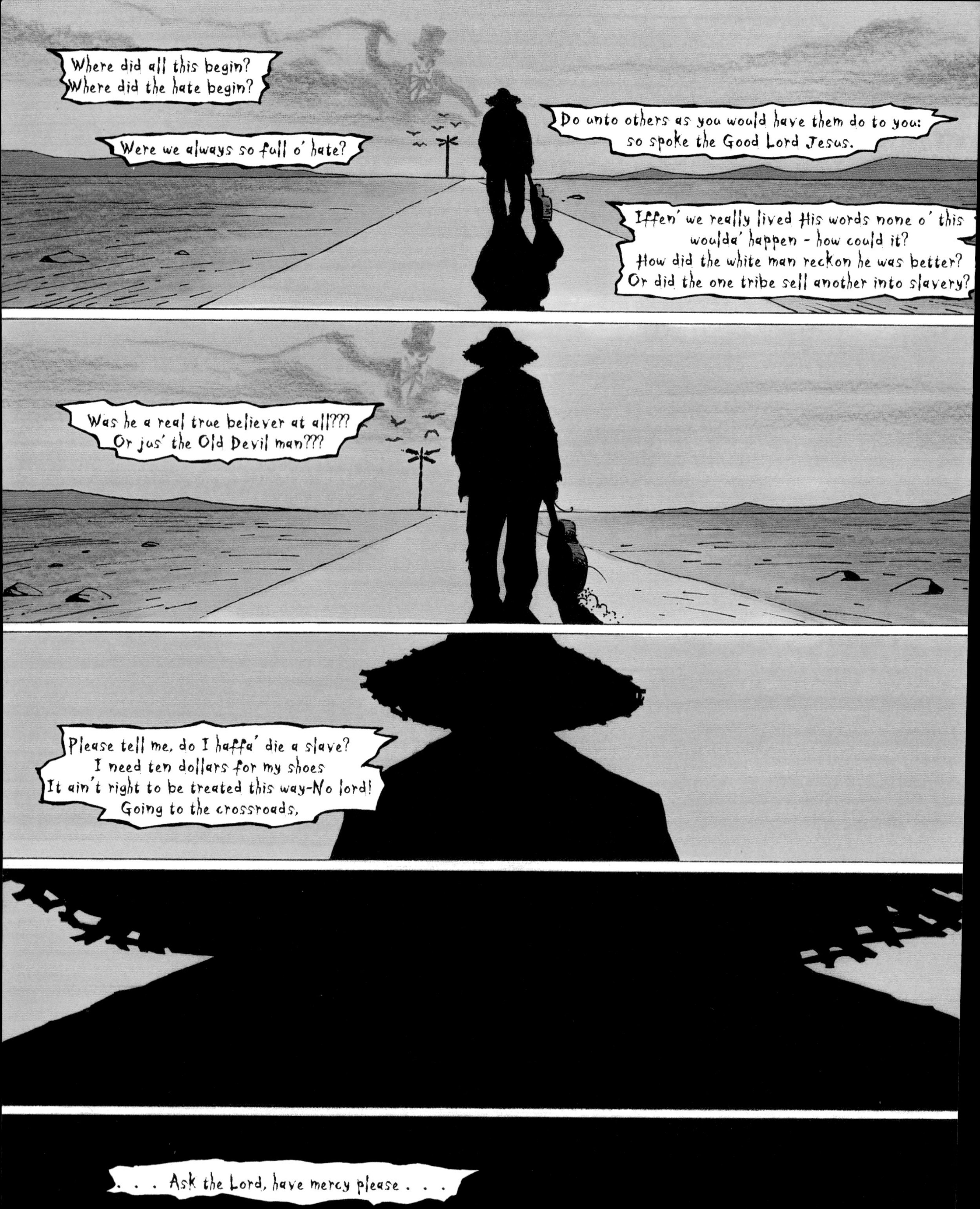
Where did all this begin?
Where did the hate begin?
Were we always so full o' hate?
Do unto others as you would have them do to you: so spoke the Good Lord Jesus.
Iffen' we really lived His words none o' this woulda' happen - how could it?
How did the white man reckon he was better?
Or did the one tribe sell another into slavery?
Was he a real true believer at all???
Or jus' the Old Devil man???
Please tell me, do I haffa' die a slave?
I need ten dollars for my shoes
It ain't right to be treated this way-No lord!
Going to the crossroads,
. . . Ask the Lord, have mercy please . . .

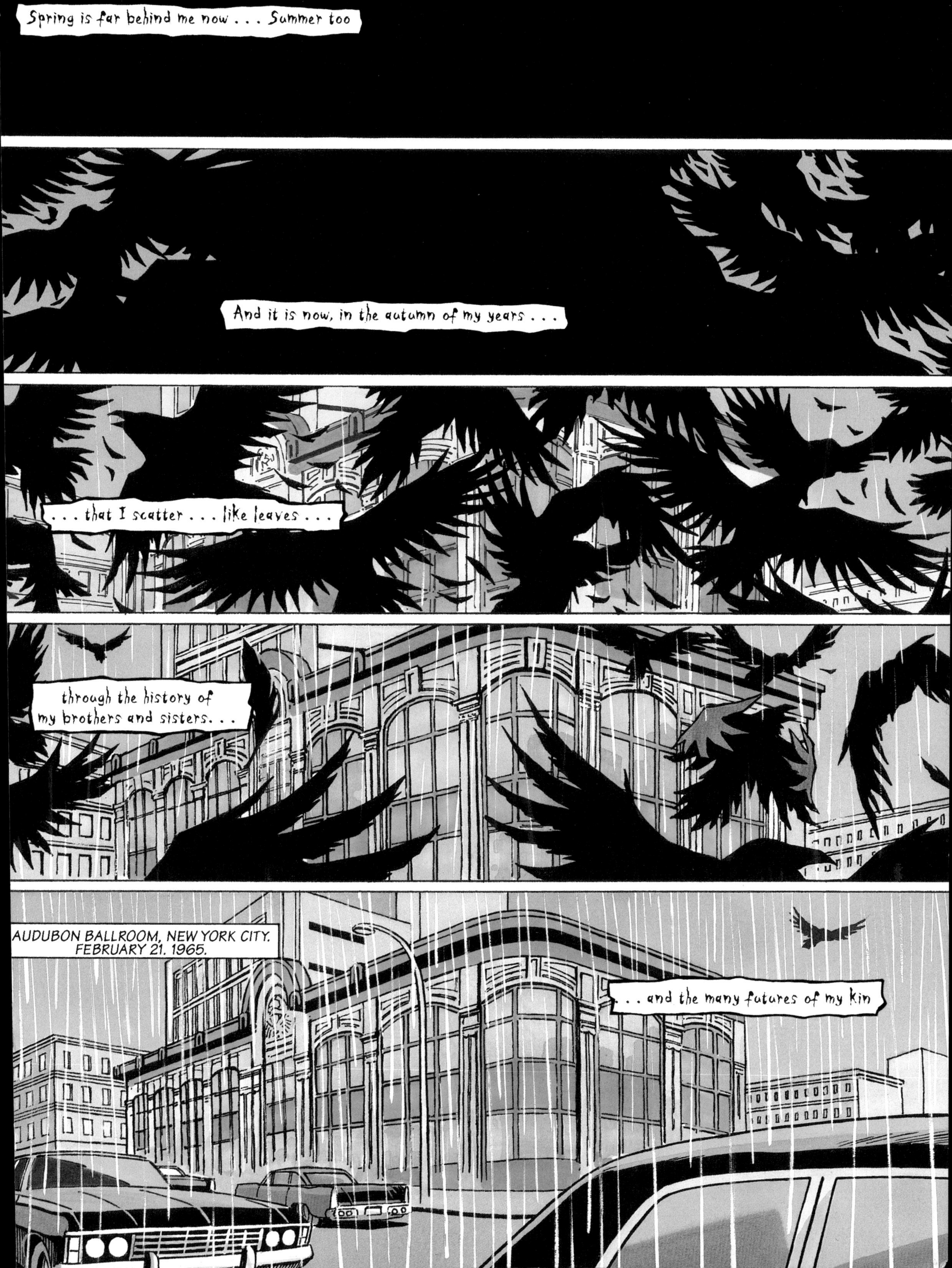

Spring is far behind me now . . . Summer too
And it is now, in the autumn of my years . . .
. . . that I scatter . . . like leaves . . .
through the history of my brothers and sisters. . .
AUDUBON BALLROOM, NEW YORK CITY. FEBRUARY 21. 1965.
. . . and the many futures of my kin

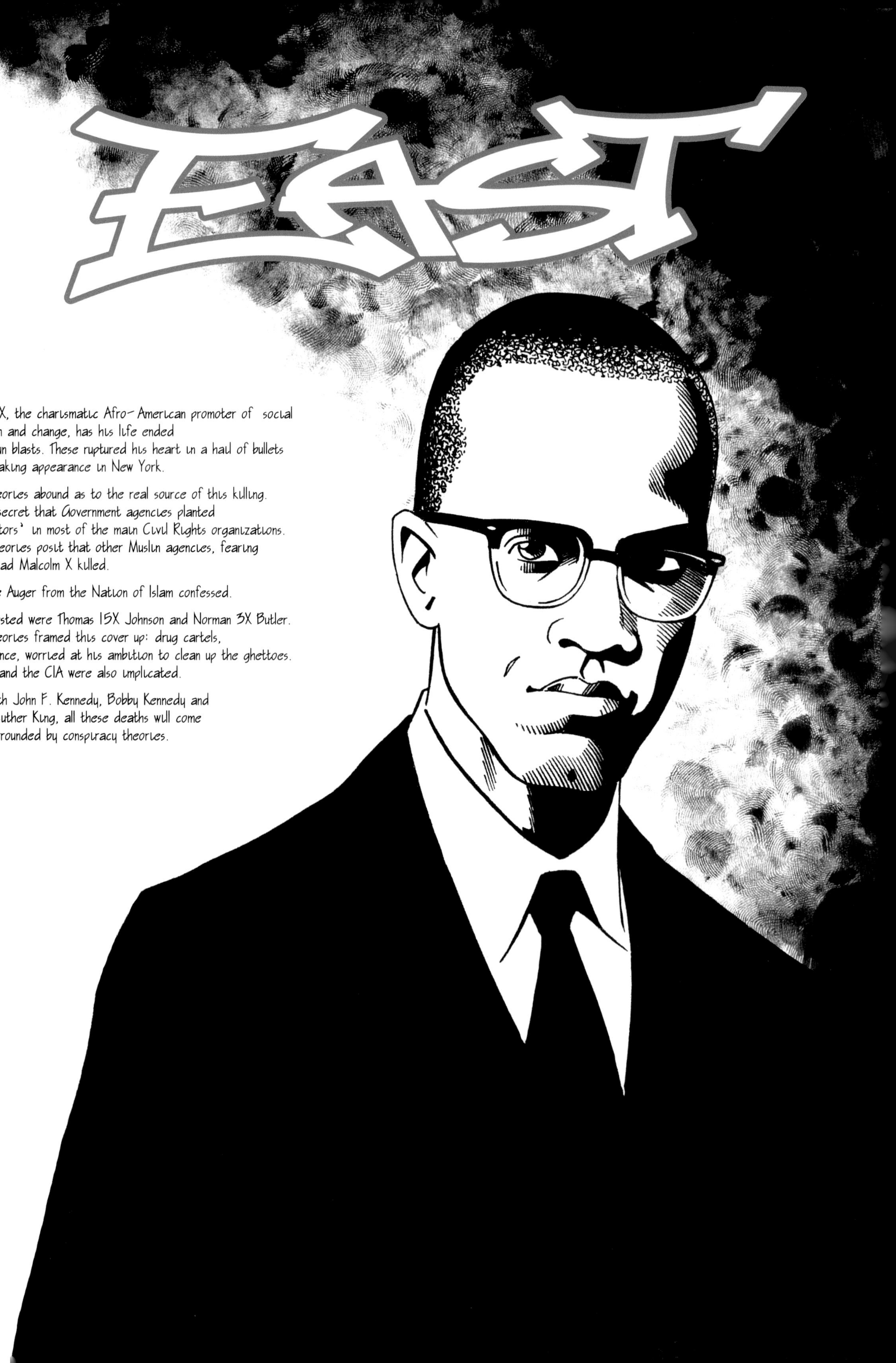
EAST

Malcolm X, the charismatic Afro-American promoter of social revolution and change, has his life ended by shotgun blasts. These ruptured his heart in a hail of bullets at a speaking appearance in New York.

Many theories abound as to the real source of this killing. It is no secret that Government agencies planted 'infiltrators' in most of the main Civil Rights organizations. Other theories posit that other Muslin agencies, fearing rivalry, had Malcolm X killed.

Talmadge Auger from the Nation of Islam confessed.

Also arrested were Thomas 15X Johnson and Norman 3X Butler. Many theories framed this cover up: drug cartels, for instance, worried at his ambition to clean up the ghettoes. The FBI and the CIA were also implicated.

Along with John F. Kennedy, Bobby Kennedy and Martin Luther King, all these deaths will come to be surrounded by conspiracy theories.

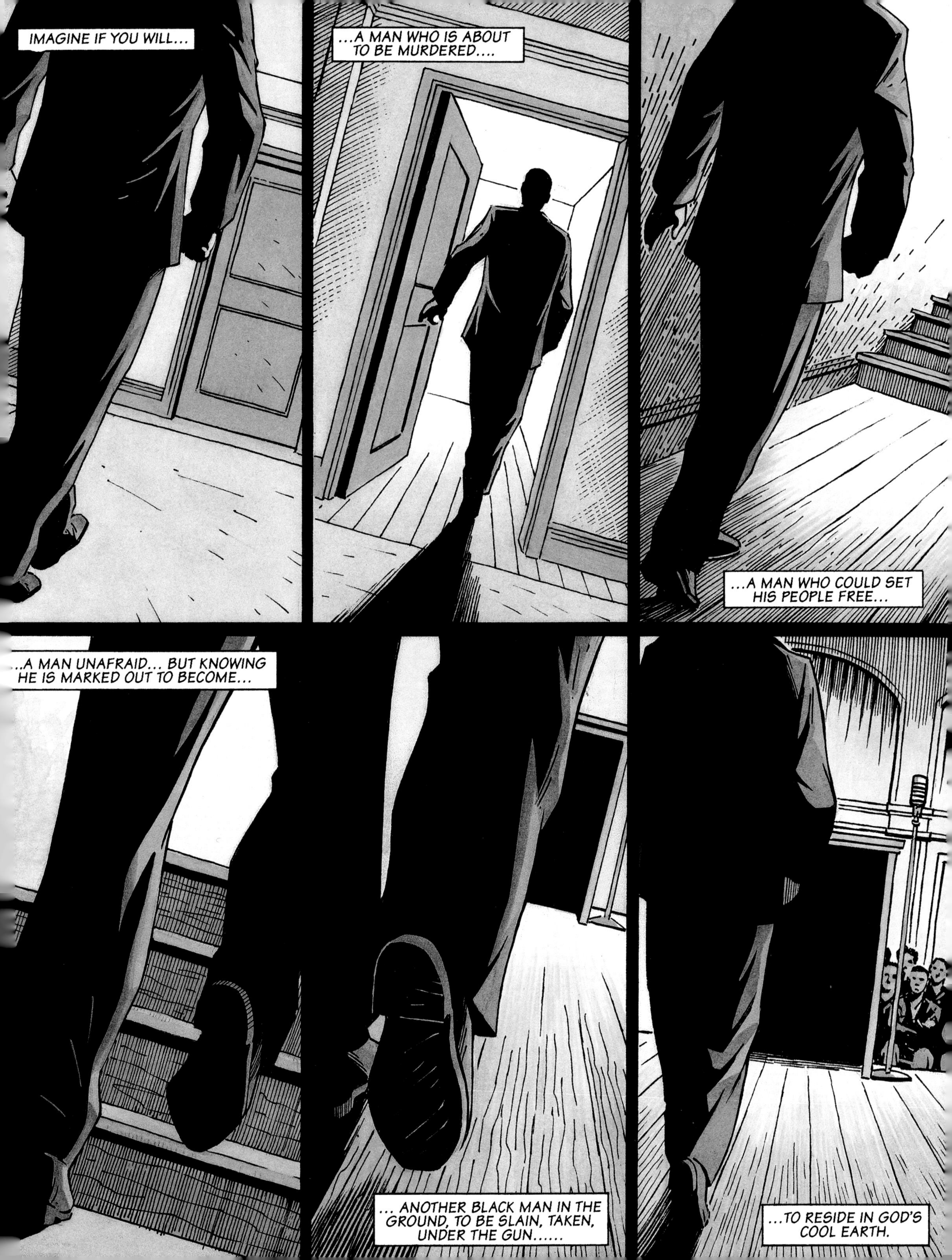
IMAGINE IF YOU WILL...
...A MAN WHO IS ABOUT TO BE MURDERED....
...A MAN WHO COULD SET HIS PEOPLE FREE...
...A MAN UNAFRAID... BUT KNOWING HE IS MARKED OUT TO BECOME...
... ANOTHER BLACK MAN IN THE GROUND, TO BE SLAIN, TAKEN, UNDER THE GUN......
...TO RESIDE IN GOD'S COOL EARTH.

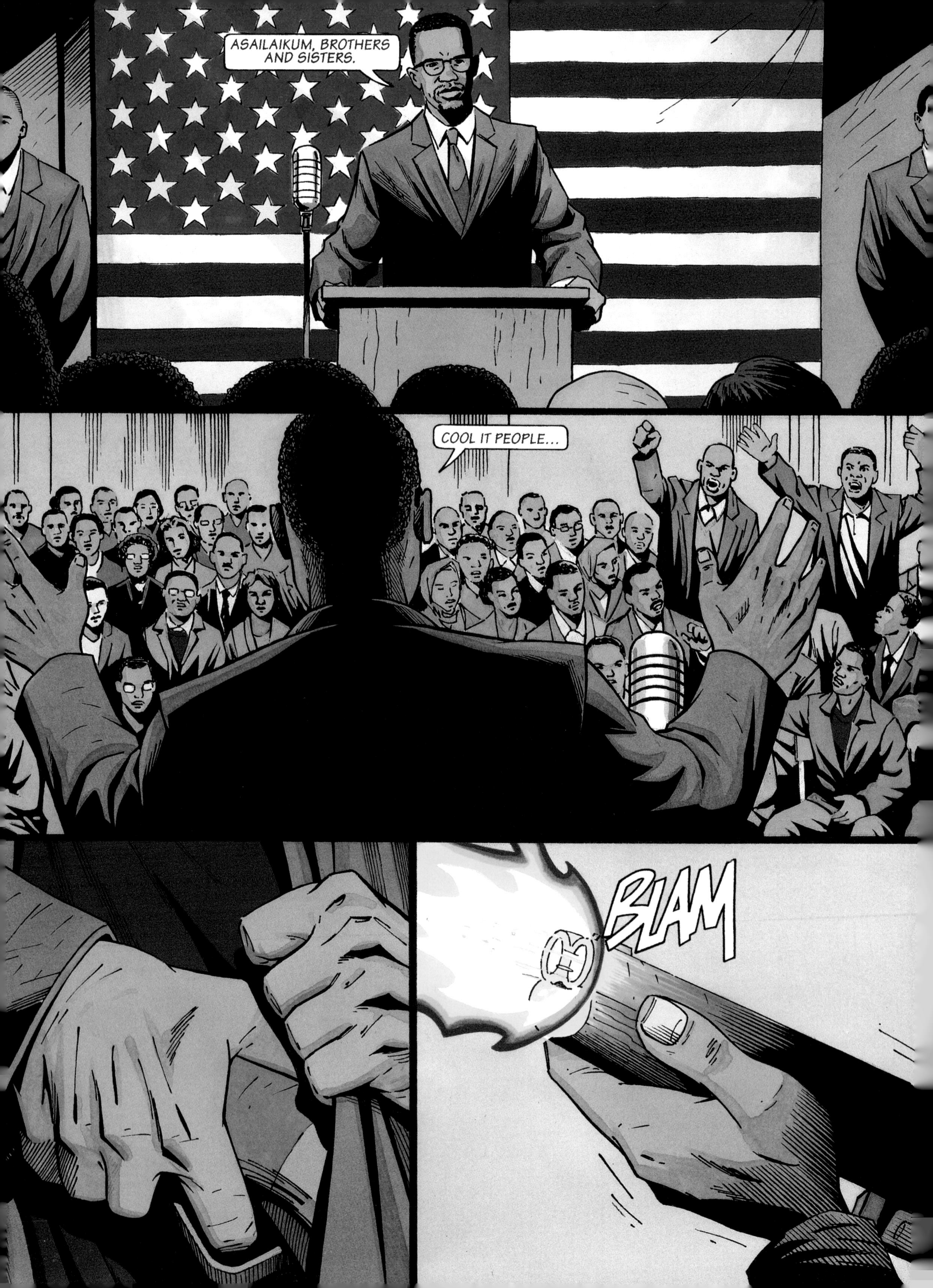
ASAILAIKUM, BROTHERS AND SISTERS.
COOL IT PEOPLE...
BLAM

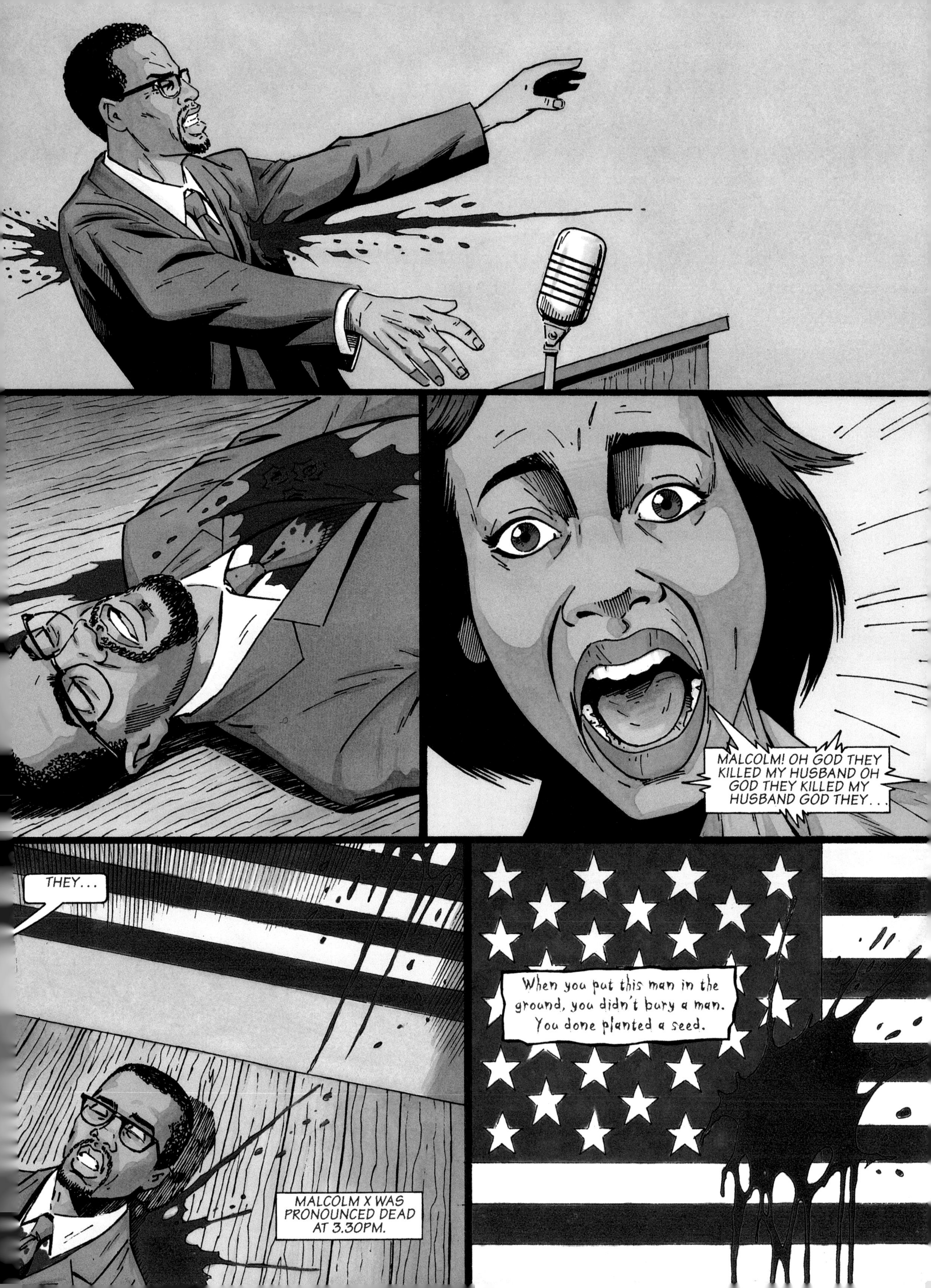
MALCOLM! OH GOD THEY KILLED MY HUSBAND OH GOD THEY KILLED MY HUSBAND GOD THEY...
THEY...
MALCOLM X WAS PRONOUNCED DEAD AT 3.30PM.
When you put this man in the ground, you didn't bury a man. You done planted a seed.

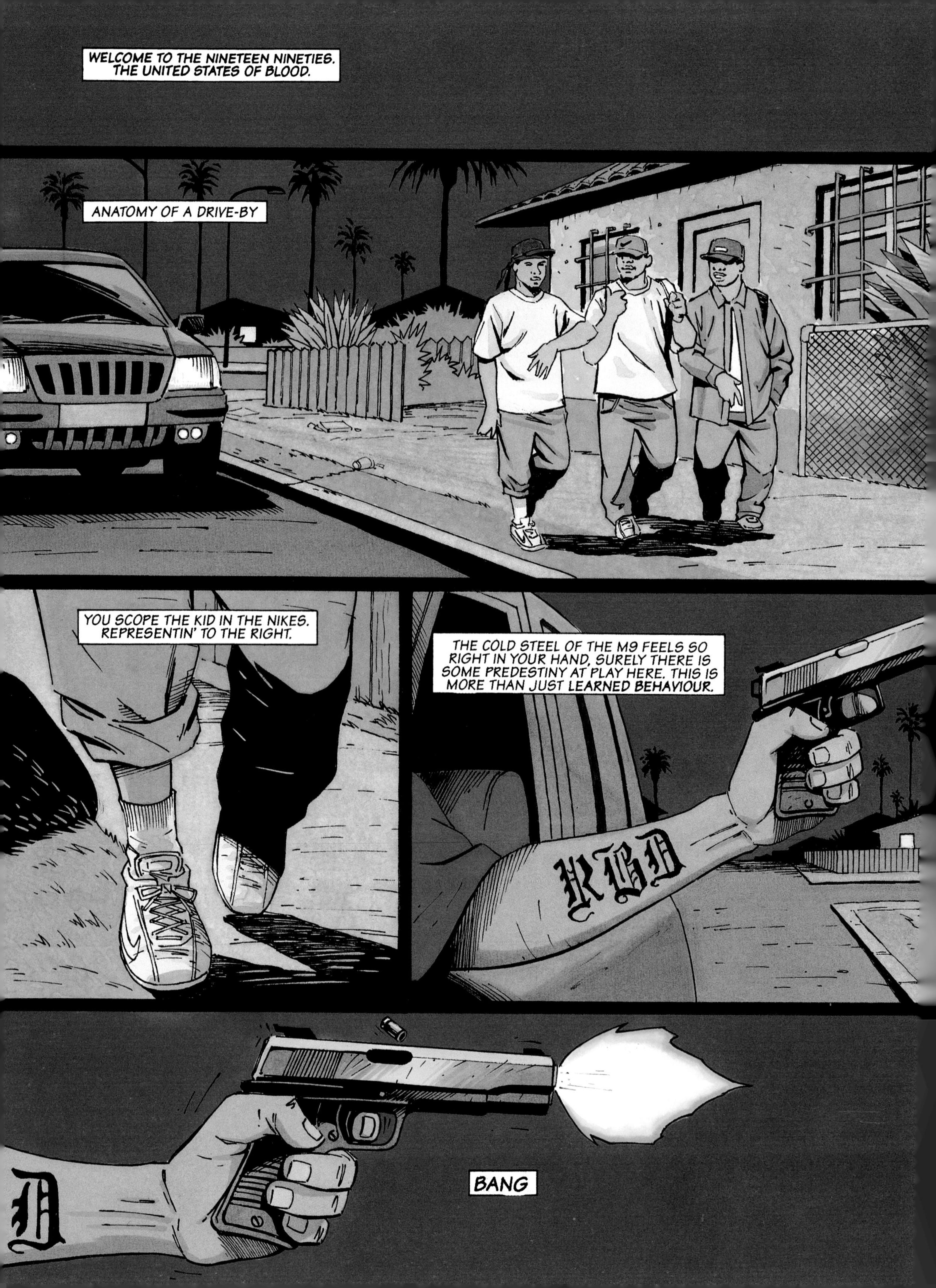
WELCOME TO THE NINETEEN NINETIES. THE UNITED STATES OF BLOOD.
ANATOMY OF A DRIVE-BY
YOU SCOPE THE KID IN THE NIKES. REPRESENTIN' TO THE RIGHT.
THE COLD STEEL OF THE M9 FEELS SO RIGHT IN YOUR HAND, SURELY THERE IS SOME PREDESTINY AT PLAY HERE. THIS IS MORE THAN JUST LEARNED BEHAVIOUR.
RBD
BANG

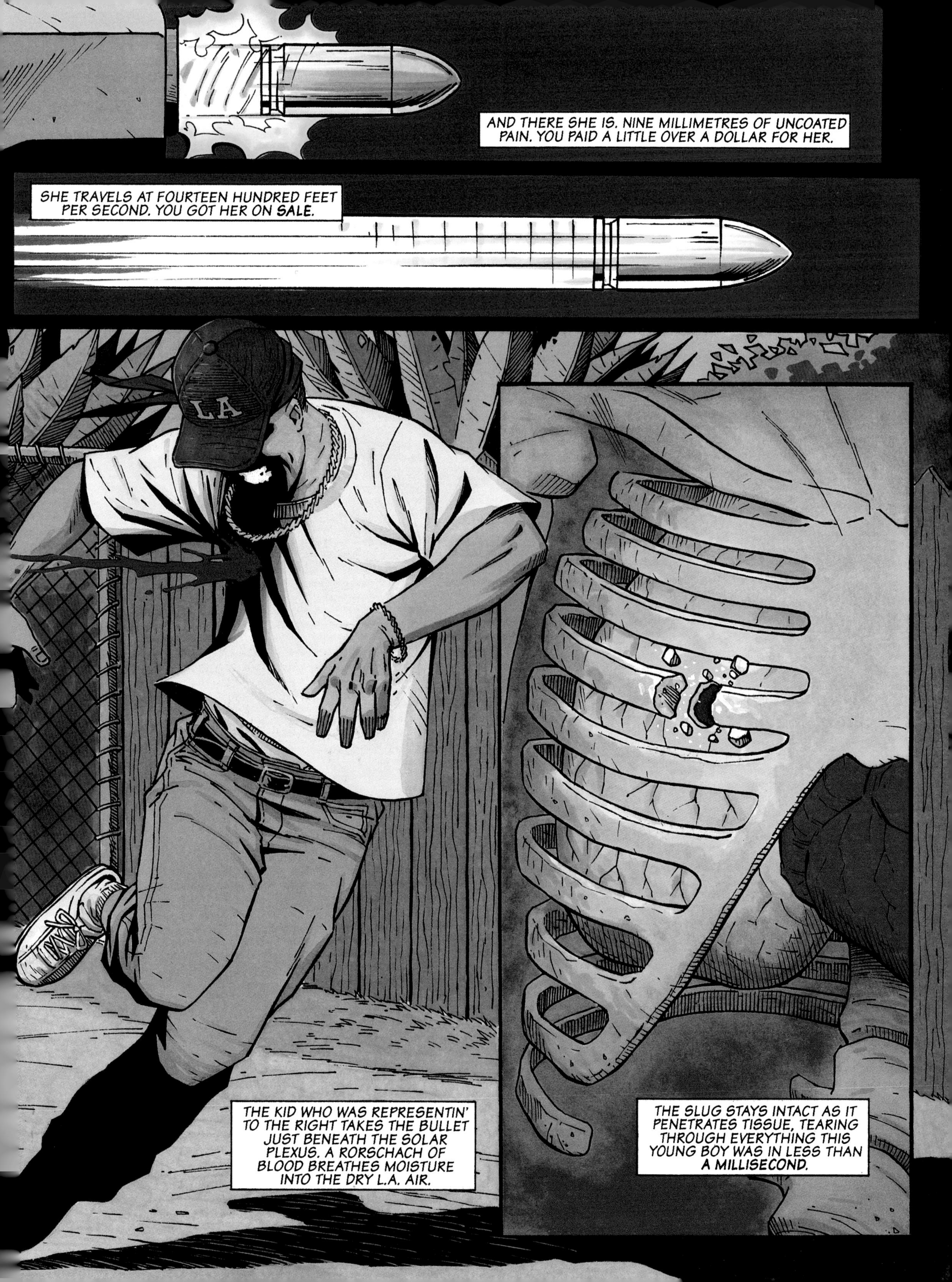
AND THERE SHE IS. NINE MILLIMETRES OF UNCOATED PAIN. YOU PAID A LITTLE OVER A DOLLAR FOR HER.
SHE TRAVELS AT FOURTEEN HUNDRED FEET PER SECOND. YOU GOT HER ON SALE.
LA
THE KID WHO WAS REPRESENTIN' TO THE RIGHT TAKES THE BULLET JUST BENEATH THE SOLAR PLEXUS. A RORSCHACH OF BLOOD BREATHES MOISTURE INTO THE DRY L.A. AIR.
THE SLUG STAYS INTACT AS IT PENETRATES TISSUE, TEARING THROUGH EVERYTHING THIS YOUNG BOY WAS IN LESS THAN A MILLISECOND.

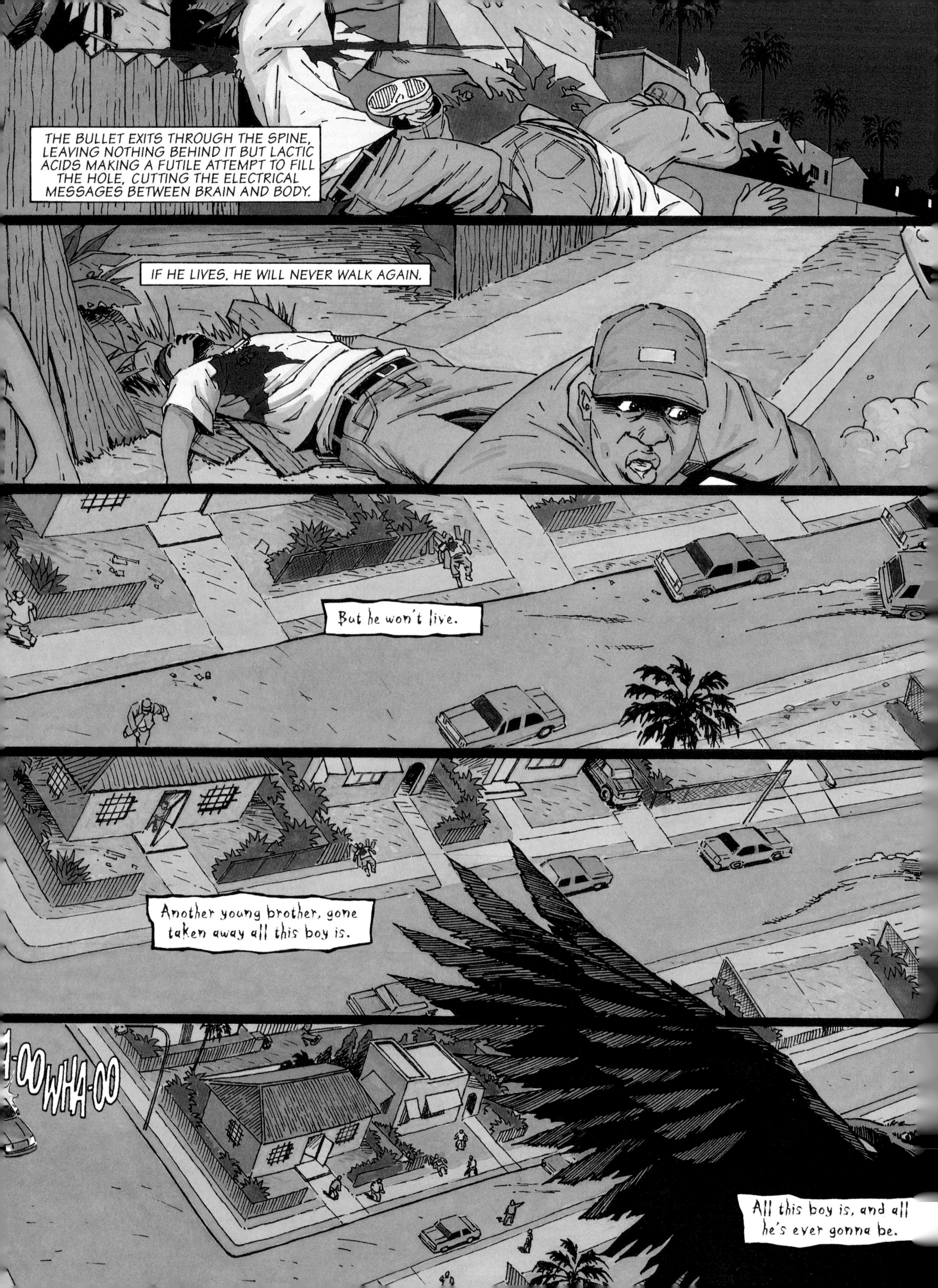
THE BULLET EXITS THROUGH THE SPINE, LEAVING NOTHING BEHIND IT BUT LACTIC ACIDS MAKING A FUTILE ATTEMPT TO FILL THE HOLE, CUTTING THE ELECTRICAL MESSAGES BETWEEN BRAIN AND BODY.
IF HE LIVES, HE WILL NEVER WALK AGAIN.
But he won't live.
Another young brother, gone taken away all this boy is.
OOWHA-OO
All this boy is, and all he's ever gonna be.

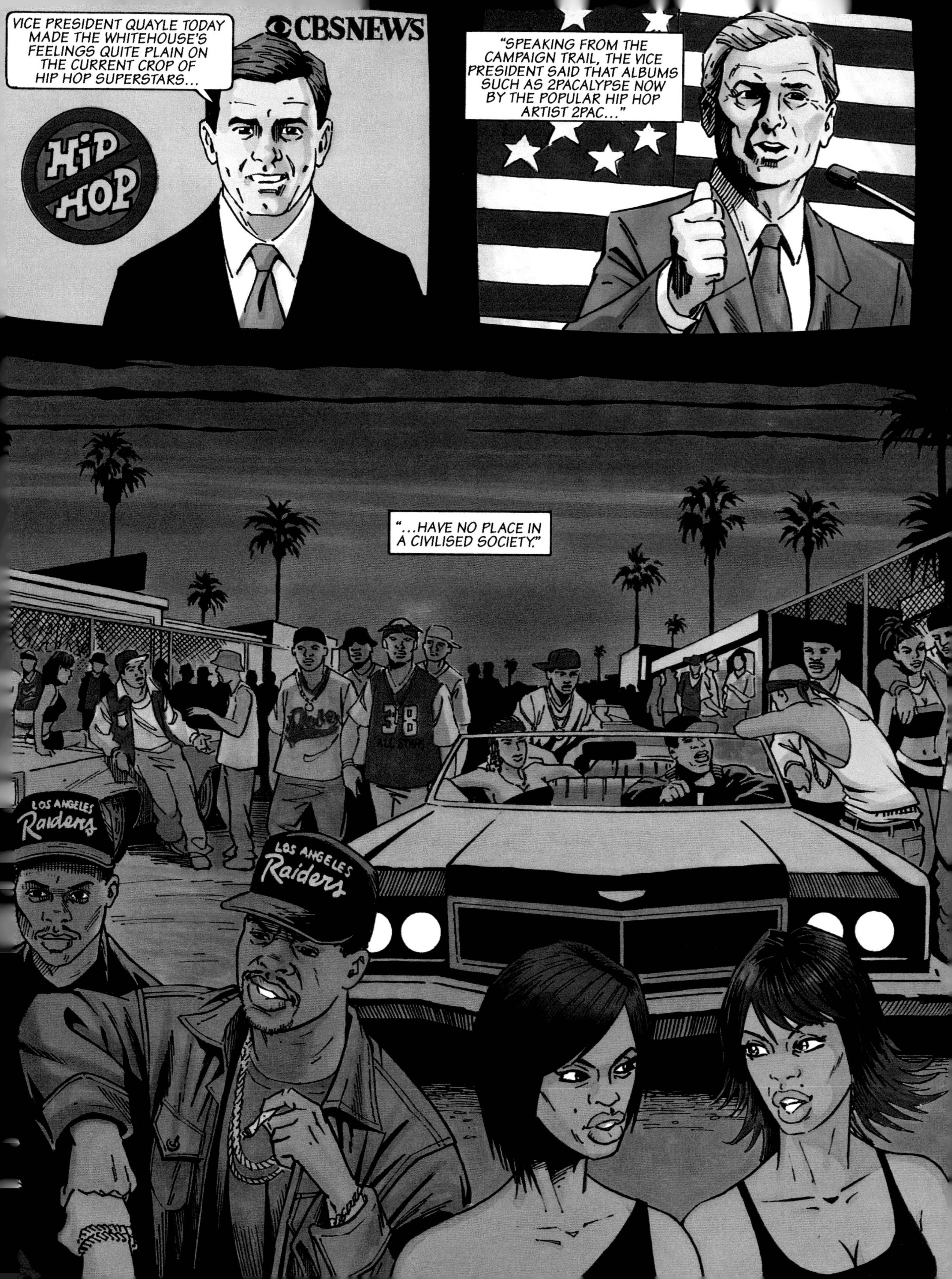
VICE PRESIDENT QUAYLE TODAY MADE THE WHITEHOUSE'S FEELINGS QUITE PLAIN ON THE CURRENT CROP OF HIP HOP SUPERSTARS...
CBSNEWS
HIP HOP
"SPEAKING FROM THE CAMPAIGN TRAIL, THE VICE PRESIDENT SAID THAT ALBUMS SUCH AS 2PACALYPSE NOW BY THE POPULAR HIP HOP ARTIST 2PAC..."
"...HAVE NO PLACE IN A CIVILISED SOCIETY."
LOS ANGELES Raiders
LOS ANGELES Raiders

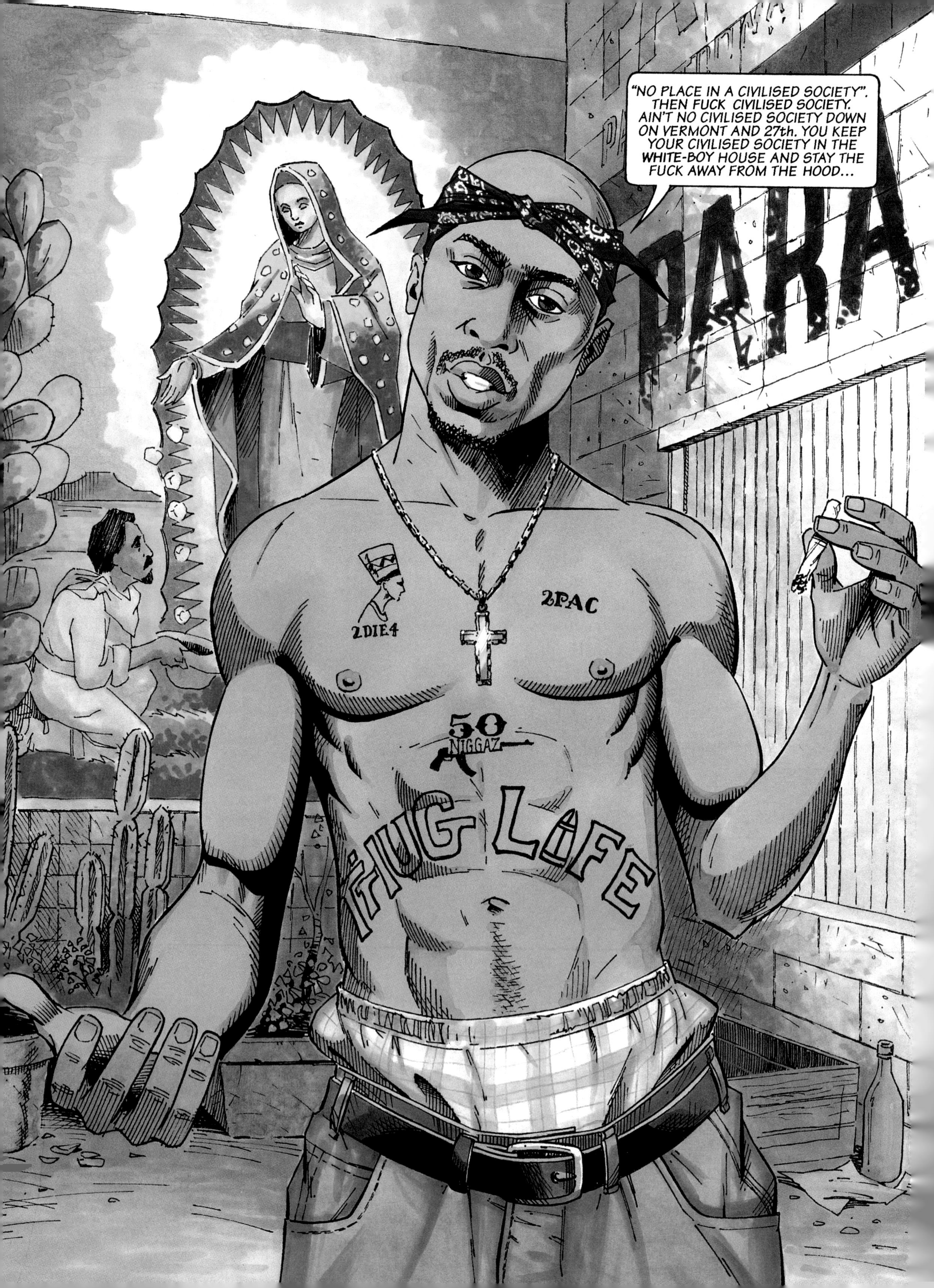
"NO PLACE IN A CIVILISED SOCIETY". THEN FUCK CIVILISED SOCIETY. AIN'T NO CIVILISED SOCIETY DOWN ON VERMONT AND 27th. YOU KEEP YOUR CIVILISED SOCIETY IN THE WHITE-BOY HOUSE AND STAY THE FUCK AWAY FROM THE HOOD...
PARA
2DIE4
2PAC
50 NIGGAZ
THUG LIFE

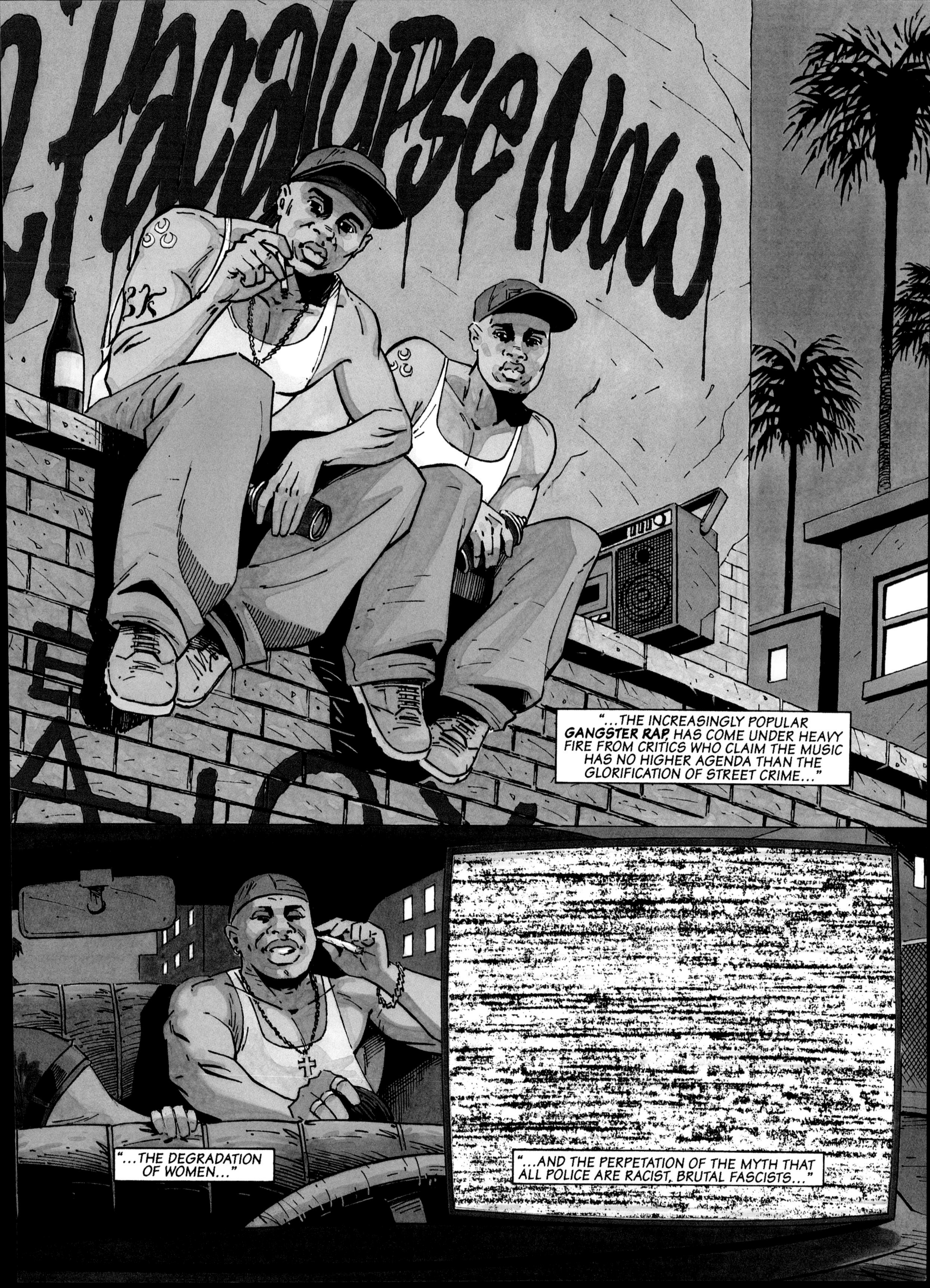
"...THE INCREASINGLY POPULAR GANGSTER RAP, HAS COME UNDER HEAVY FIRE FROM CRITICS WHO CLAIM THE MUSIC HAS NO HIGHER AGENDA THAN THE GLORIFICATION OF STREET CRIME..."
"...THE DEGRADATION OF WOMEN..."
"...AND THE PERPETATION OF THE MYTH THAT ALL POLICE ARE RACIST, BRUTAL FASCISTS..."

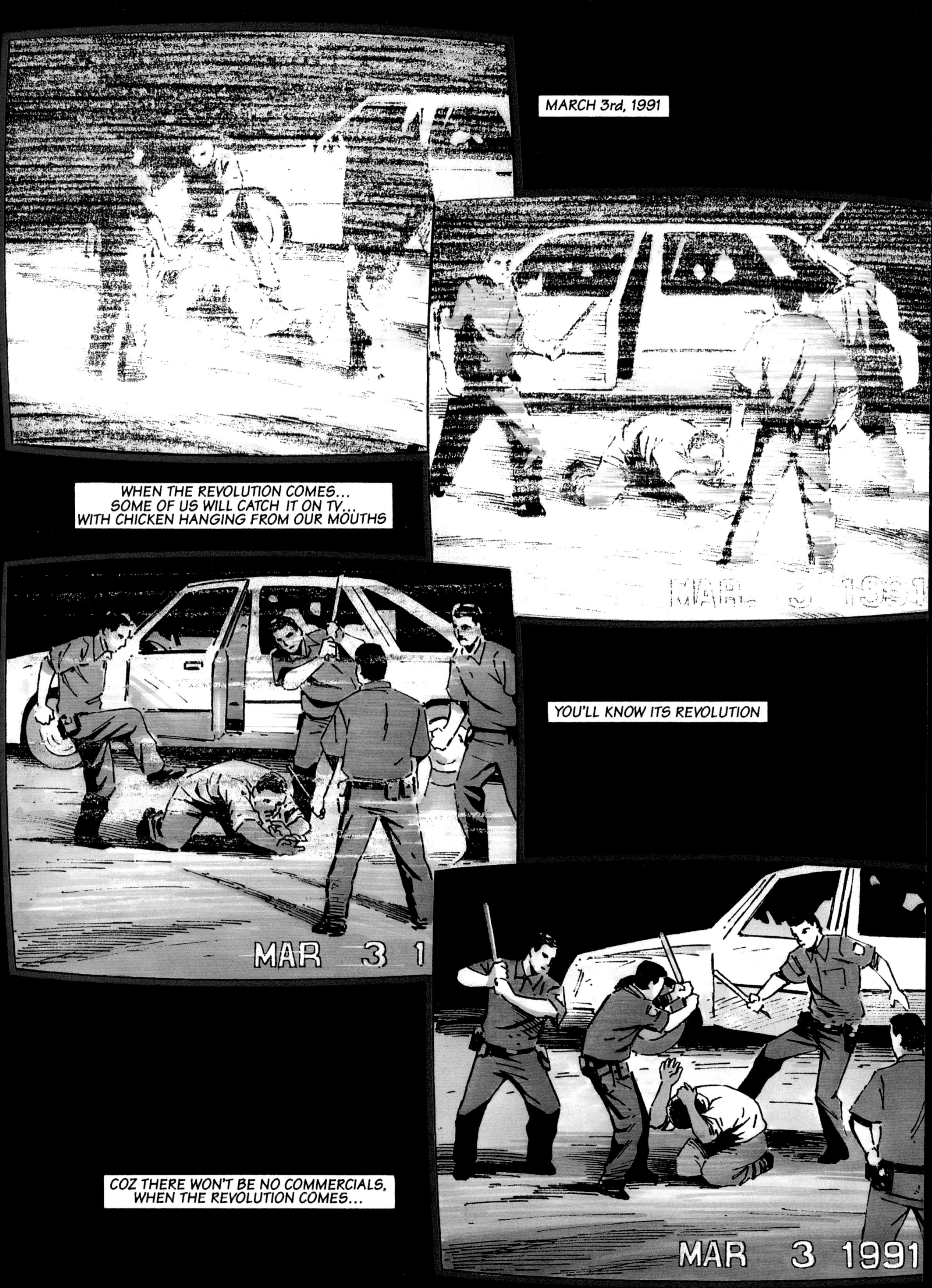
MARCH 3rd, 1991
WHEN THE REVOLUTION COMES...
SOME OF US WILL CATCH IT ON TV...
WITH CHICKEN HANGING FROM OUR MOUTHS
YOU'LL KNOW ITS REVOLUTION
MAR 3 1
COZ THERE WON'T BE NO COMMERCIALS,
WHEN THE REVOLUTION COMES...
MAR 3 1991

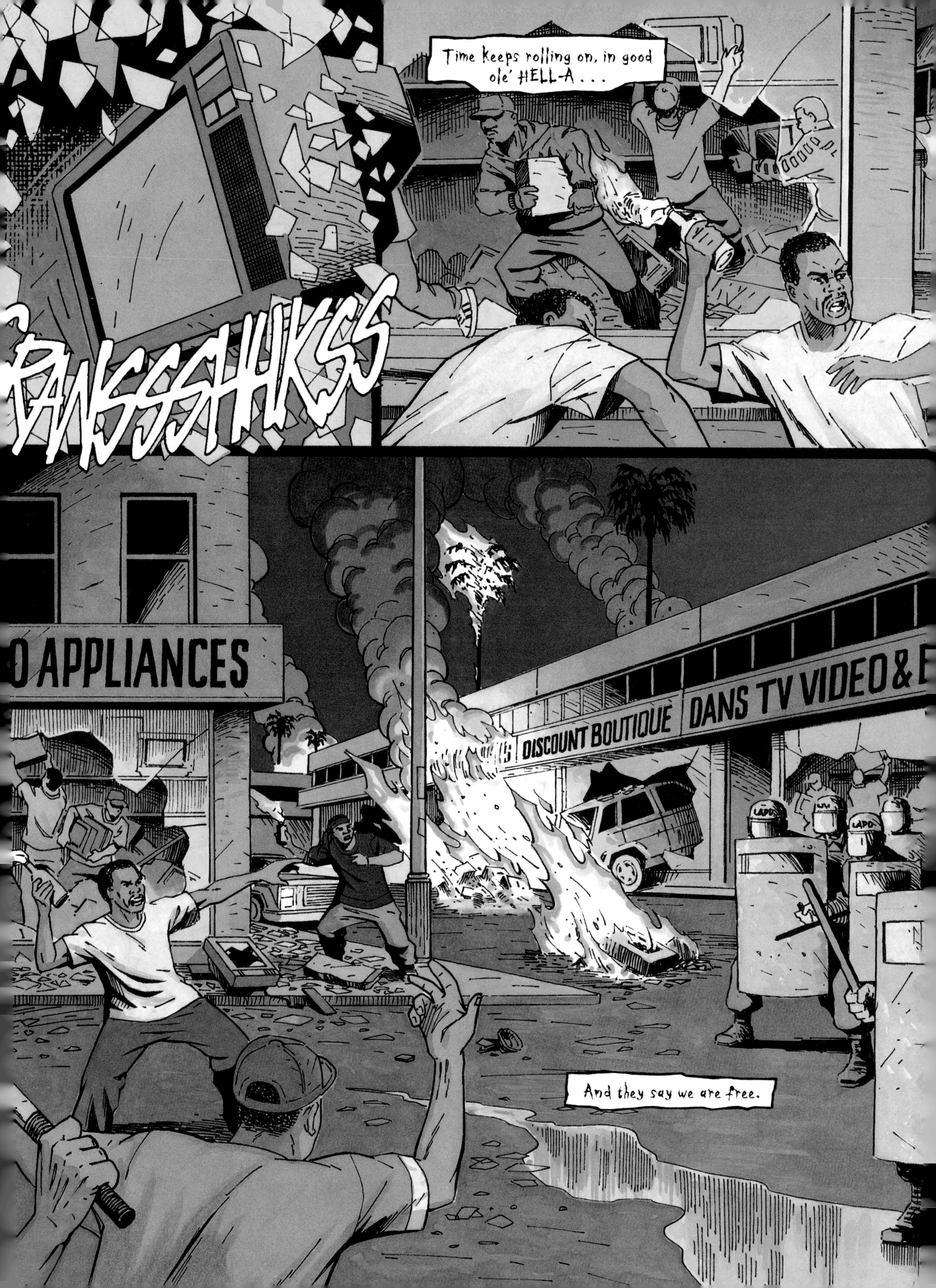
Time keeps rolling on, in good ole' HELL-A . . .
BANSSSHHKSS
O APPLIANCES
DISCOUNT BOUTIQUE
DANS TV VIDEO &
LAPD
And they say we are free.

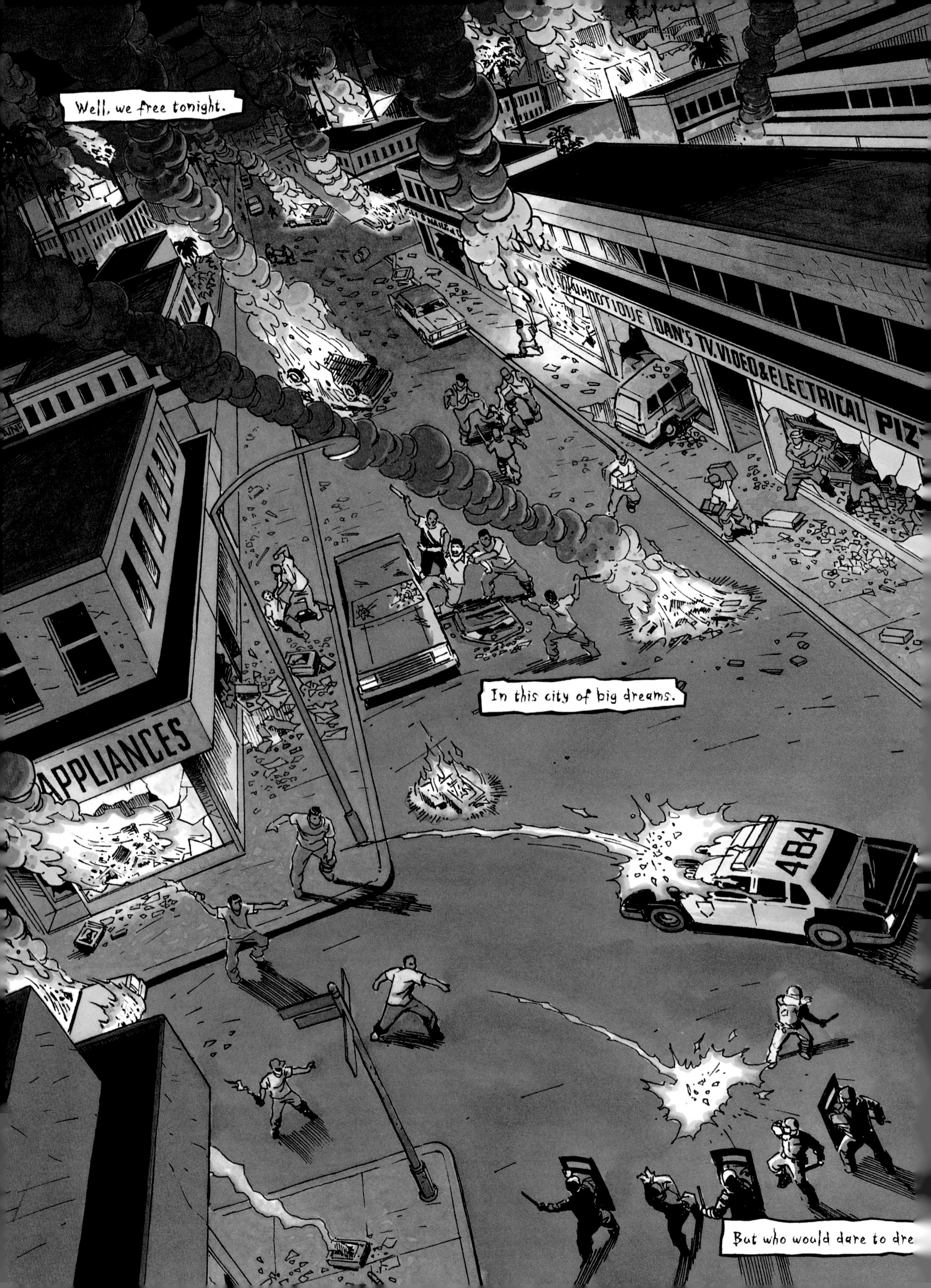
Well, we free tonight.
DAN'S TV. VIDEO & ELECTRICAL
PIZ
In this city of big dreams.
APPLIANCES
484
But who would dare to dre

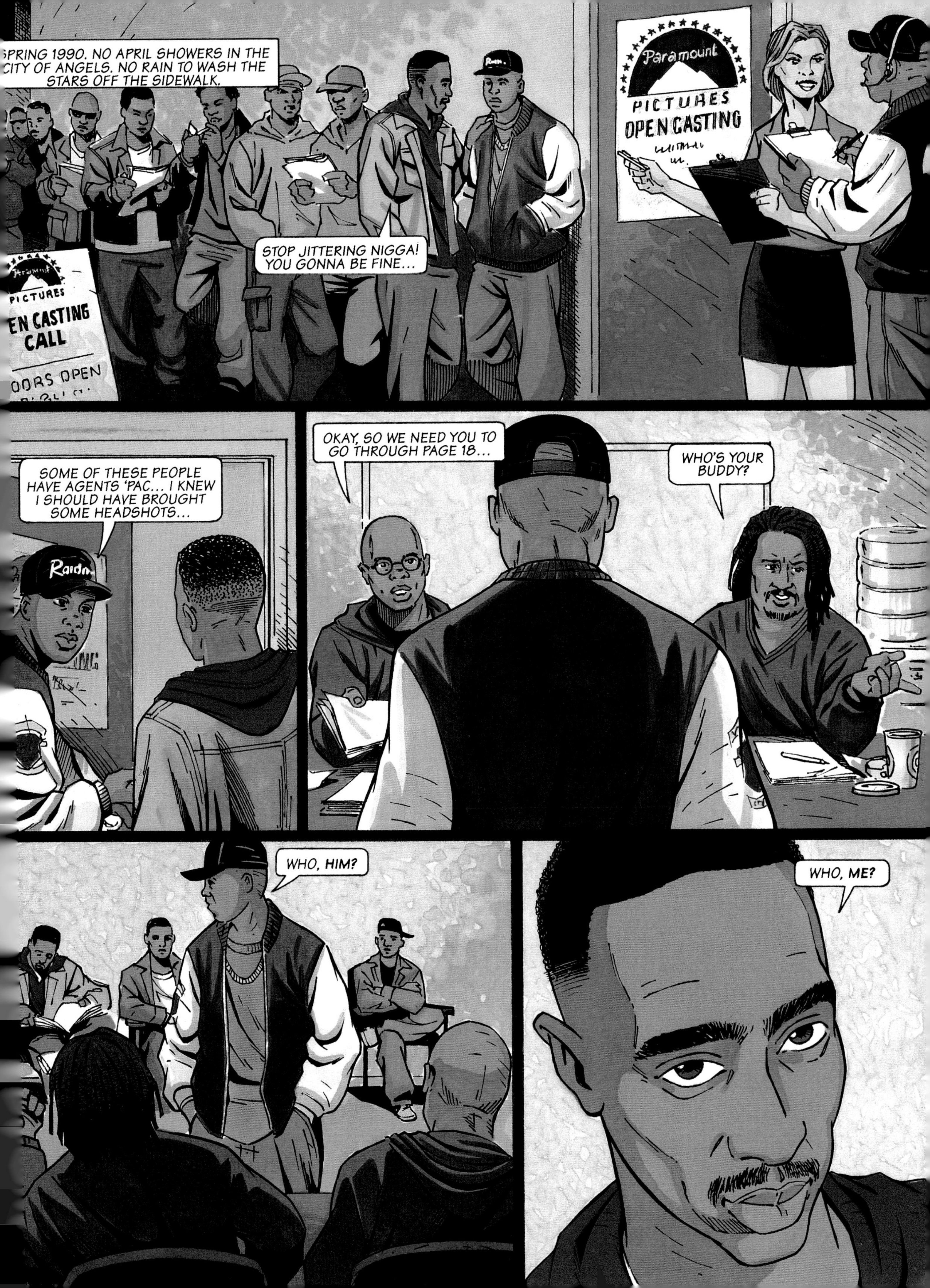

SPRING 1990. NO APRIL SHOWERS IN THE CITY OF ANGELS. NO RAIN TO WASH THE STARS OFF THE SIDEWALK.
PICTURES
EN CASTING CALL
OORS OPEN
STOP JITTERING NIGGA! YOU GONNA BE FINE...
Paramount
PICTURES
OPEN CASTING
SOME OF THESE PEOPLE HAVE AGENTS 'PAC... I KNEW I SHOULD HAVE BROUGHT SOME HEADSHOTS...
OKAY, SO WE NEED YOU TO GO THROUGH PAGE 18...
WHO'S YOUR BUDDY?
WHO, **HIM?**
WHO, **ME?**

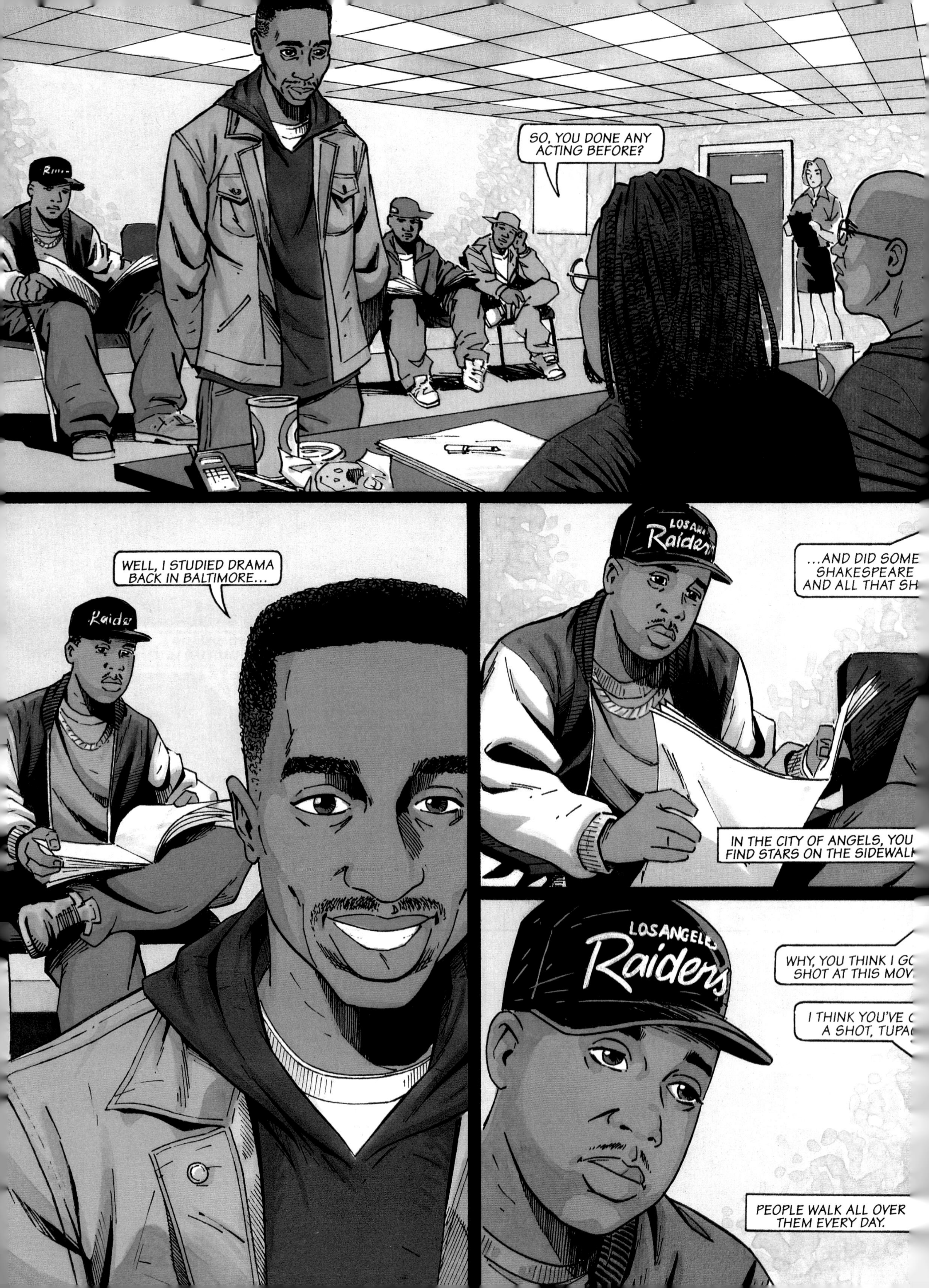
SO, YOU DONE ANY ACTING BEFORE?
WELL, I STUDIED DRAMA BACK IN BALTIMORE...
...AND DID SOME SHAKESPEARE AND ALL THAT SH
IN THE CITY OF ANGELS, YOU FIND STARS ON THE SIDEWALK
WHY, YOU THINK I GO SHOT AT THIS MOV
I THINK YOU'VE A SHOT, TUPA
PEOPLE WALK ALL OVER THEM EVERY DAY.

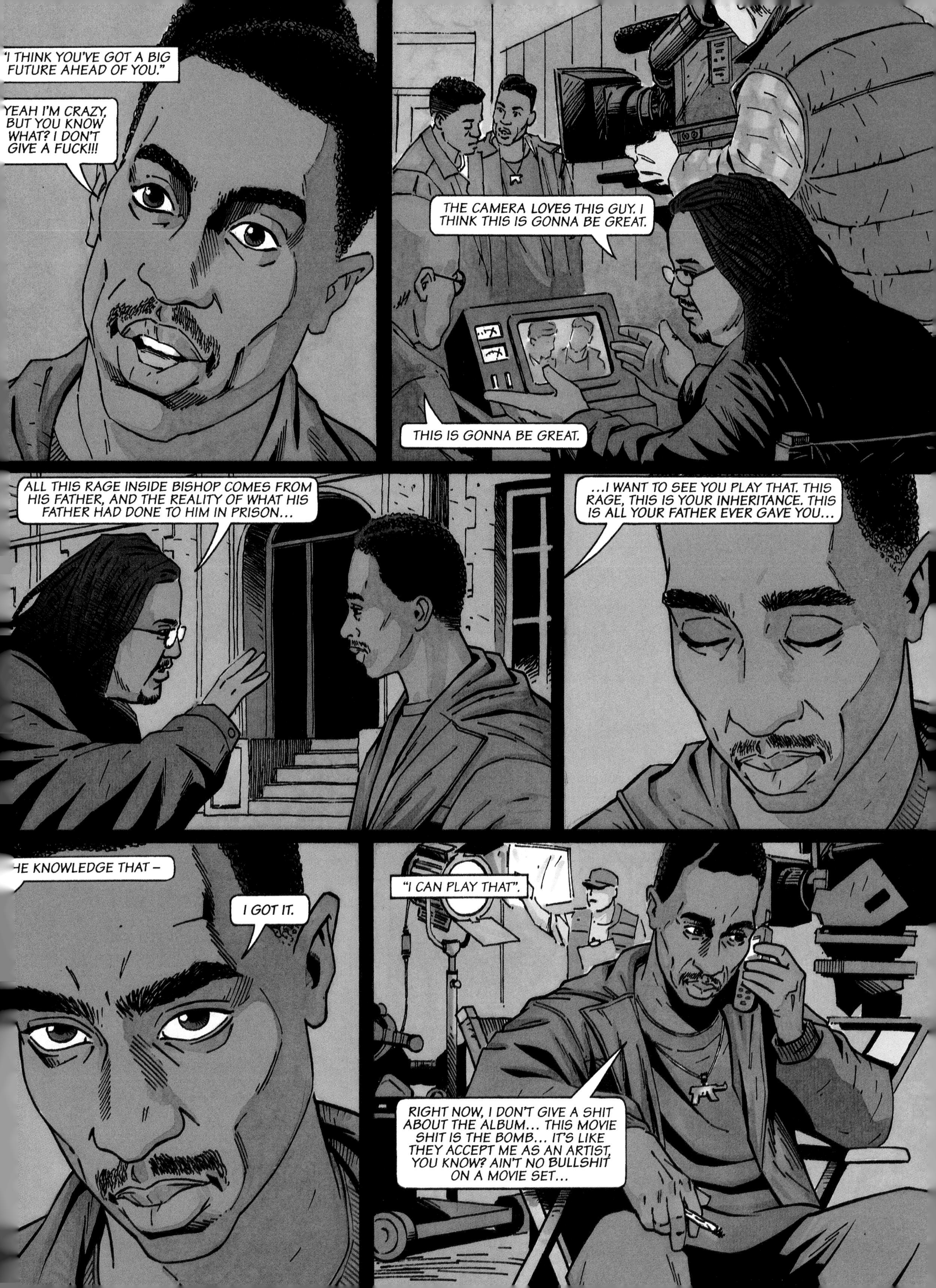
"I THINK YOU'VE GOT A BIG FUTURE AHEAD OF YOU."
YEAH I'M CRAZY, BUT YOU KNOW WHAT? I DON'T GIVE A FUCK!!!
THE CAMERA LOVES THIS GUY. I THINK THIS IS GONNA BE GREAT.
THIS IS GONNA BE GREAT.
ALL THIS RAGE INSIDE BISHOP COMES FROM HIS FATHER, AND THE REALITY OF WHAT HIS FATHER HAD DONE TO HIM IN PRISON...
...I WANT TO SEE YOU PLAY THAT. THIS RAGE, THIS IS YOUR INHERITANCE. THIS IS ALL YOUR FATHER EVER GAVE YOU...
HE KNOWLEDGE THAT –
I GOT IT.
"I CAN PLAY THAT".
RIGHT NOW, I DON'T GIVE A SHIT ABOUT THE ALBUM... THIS MOVIE SHIT IS THE BOMB... IT'S LIKE THEY ACCEPT ME AS AN ARTIST, YOU KNOW? AIN'T NO BULLSHIT ON A MOVIE SET...

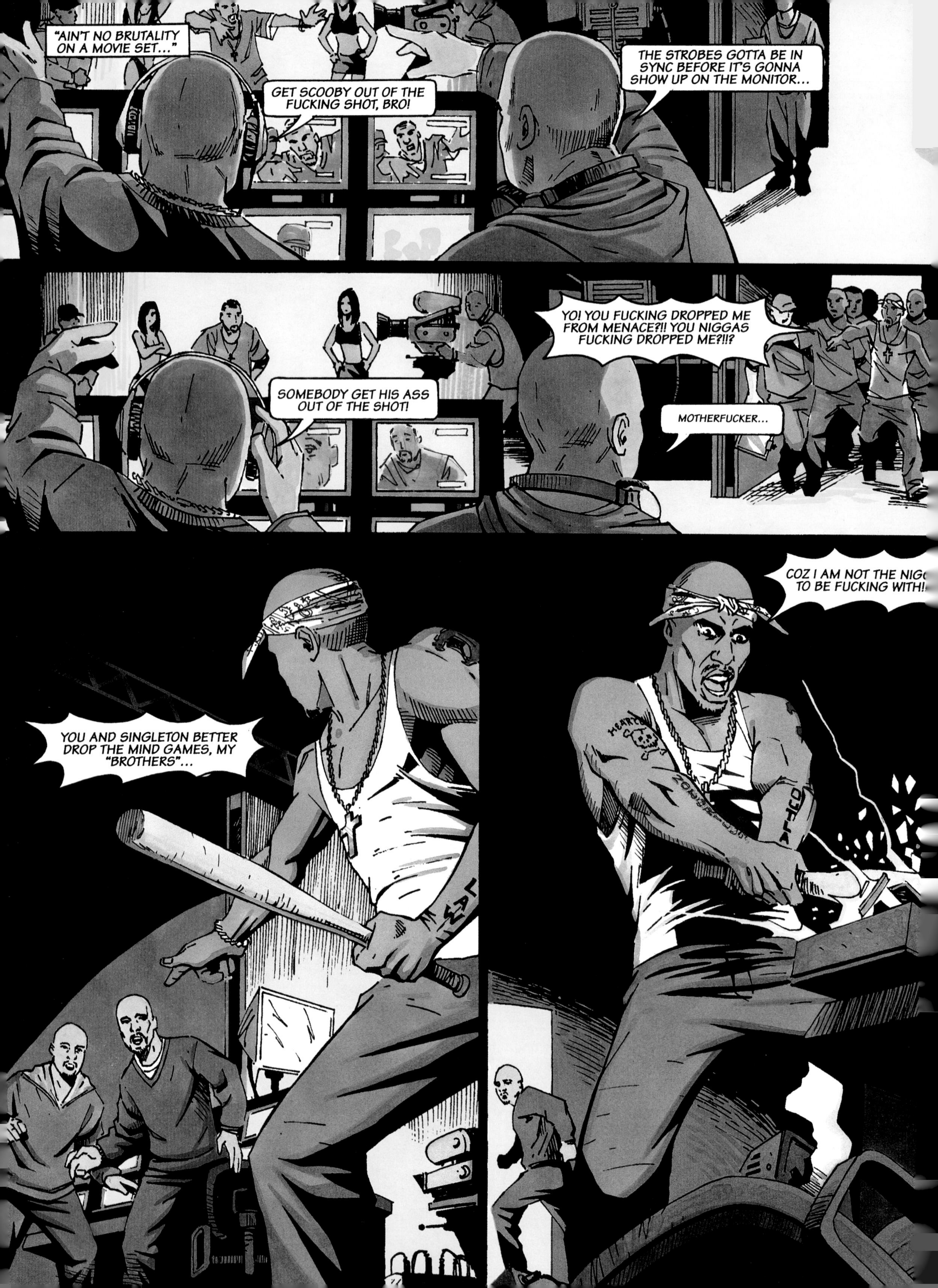
"AIN'T NO BRUTALITY ON A MOVIE SET..."
GET SCOOBY OUT OF THE FUCKING SHOT, BRO!
THE STROBES GOTTA BE IN SYNC BEFORE IT'S GONNA SHOW UP ON THE MONITOR...
YO! YOU FUCKING DROPPED ME FROM MENACE?!! YOU NIGGAS FUCKING DROPPED ME?!!?
SOMEBODY GET HIS ASS OUT OF THE SHOT!
MOTHERFUCKER...
YOU AND SINGLETON BETTER DROP THE MIND GAMES, MY "BROTHERS"...
COZ I AM NOT THE NIG
TO BE FUCKING WITH!

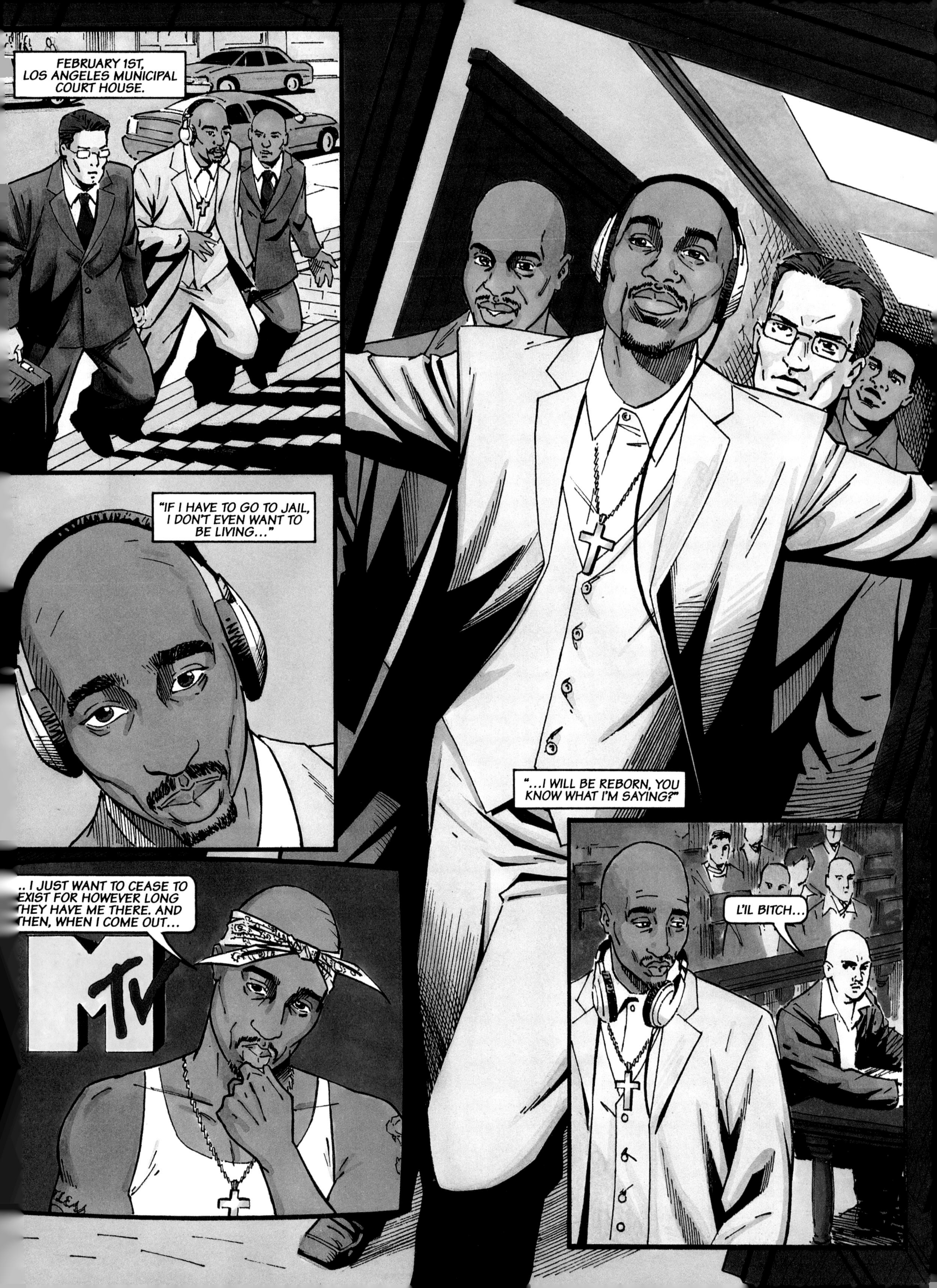

FEBRUARY 1ST, LOS ANGELES MUNICIPAL COURT HOUSE.
"IF I HAVE TO GO TO JAIL, I DON'T EVEN WANT TO BE LIVING..."
.. I JUST WANT TO CEASE TO EXIST FOR HOWEVER LONG THEY HAVE ME THERE. AND THEN, WHEN I COME OUT...
"...I WILL BE REBORN, YOU KNOW WHAT I'M SAYING?"
L'IL BITCH...

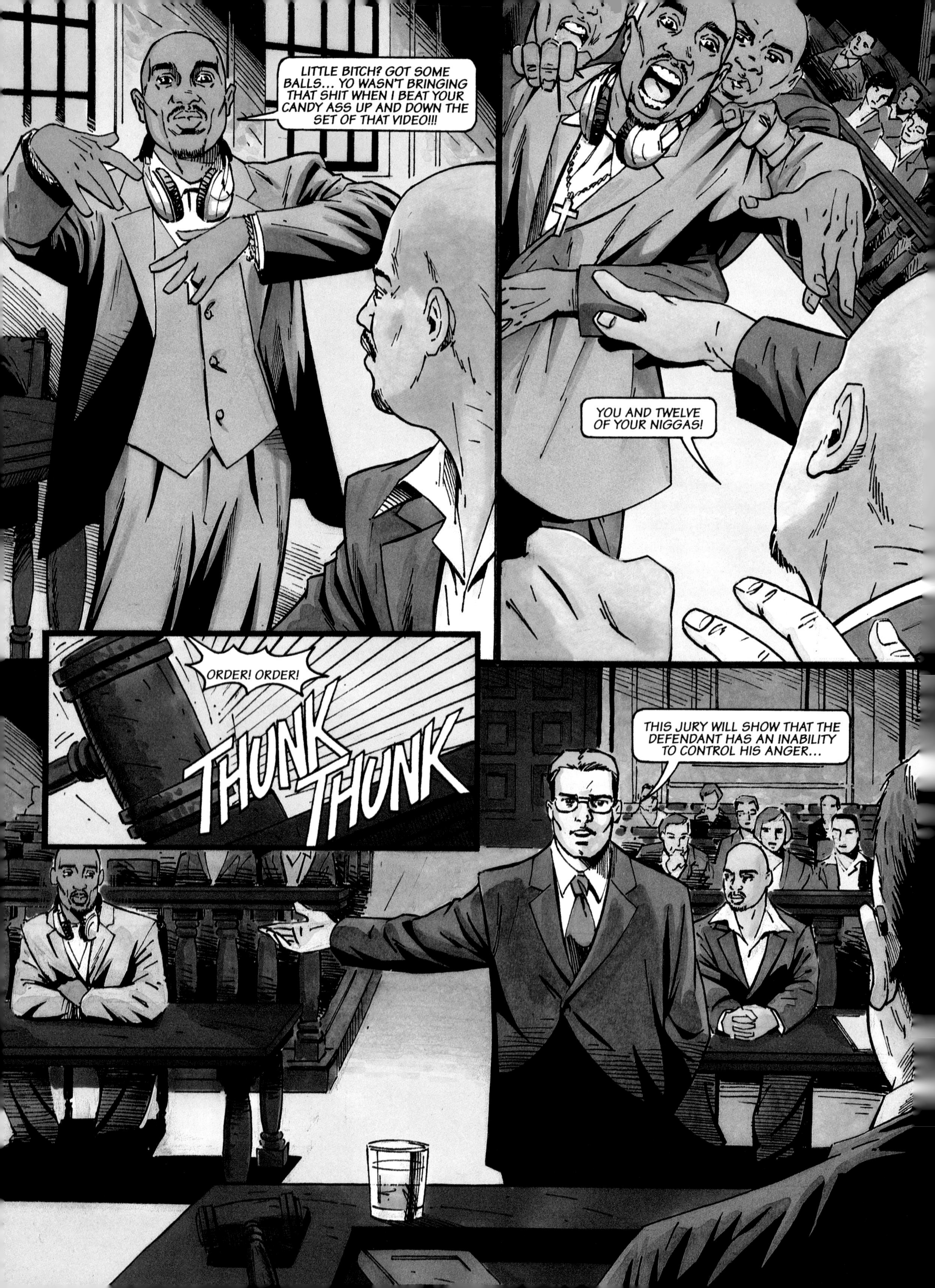
LITTLE BITCH? GOT SOME BALLS... YO WASN'T BRINGING THAT SHIT WHEN I BEAT YOUR CANDY ASS UP AND DOWN THE SET OF THAT VIDEO!!!
YOU AND TWELVE OF YOUR NIGGAS!
ORDER! ORDER!
THUNK THUNK
THIS JURY WILL SHOW THAT THE DEFENDANT HAS AN INABILITY TO CONTROL HIS ANGER...

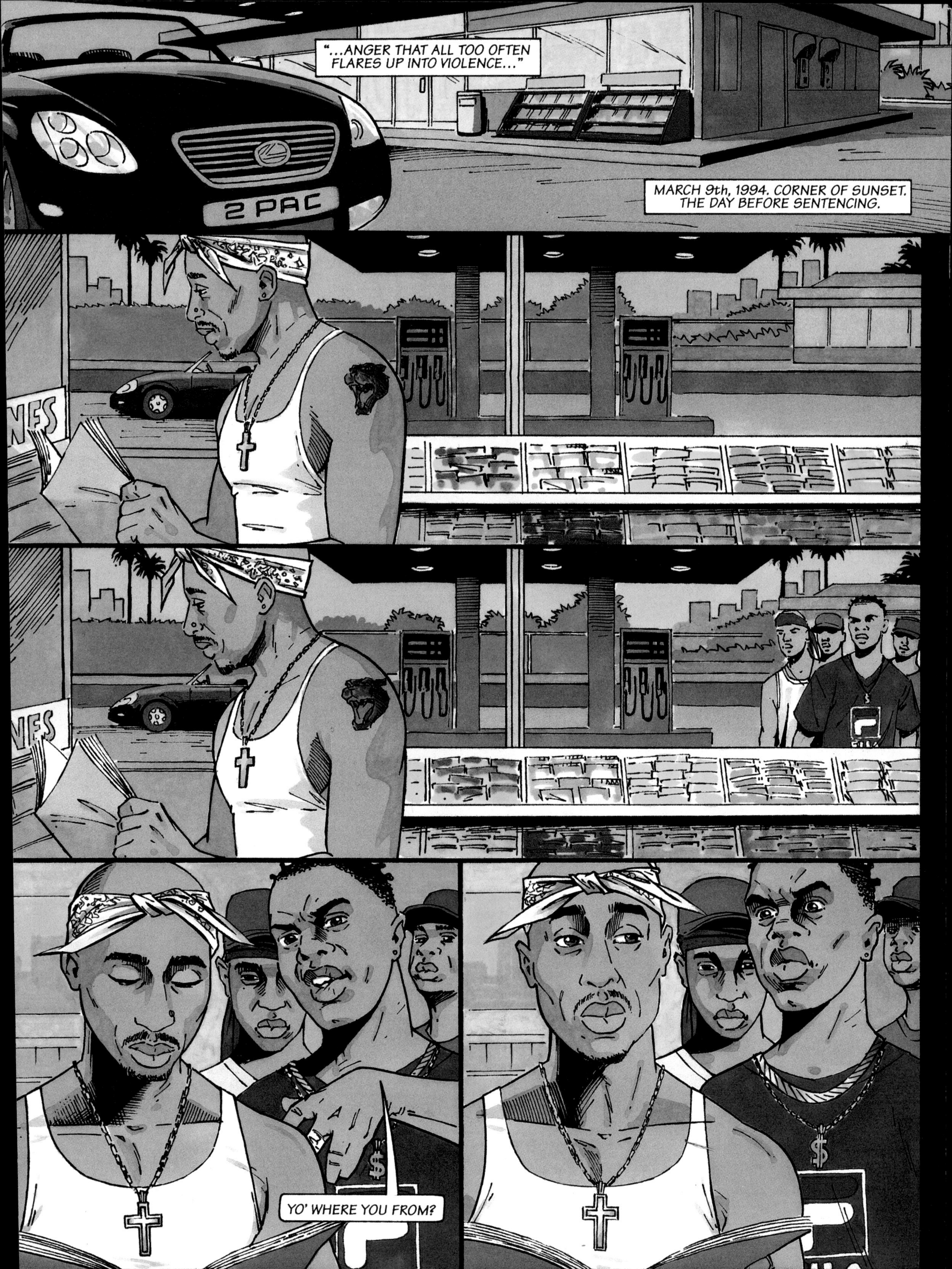
"...ANGER THAT ALL TOO OFTEN FLARES UP INTO VIOLENCE..."
2 PAC
MARCH 9th, 1994. CORNER OF SUNSET. THE DAY BEFORE SENTENCING.
YO' WHERE YOU FROM?

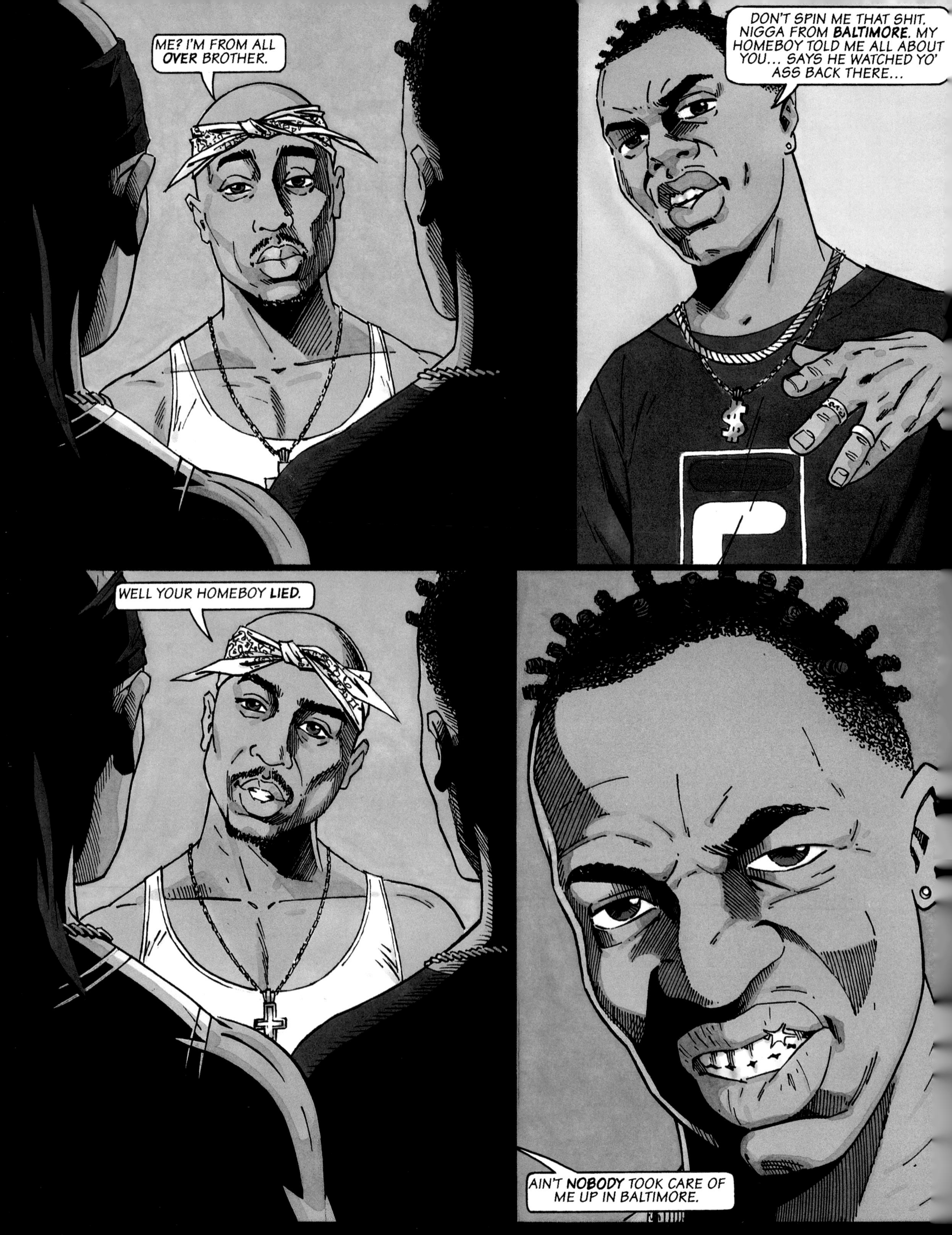
ME? I'M FROM ALL OVER BROTHER.
DON'T SPIN ME THAT SHIT. NIGGA FROM BALTIMORE. MY HOMEBOY TOLD ME ALL ABOUT YOU... SAYS HE WATCHED YO' ASS BACK THERE...
WELL YOUR HOMEBOY LIED.
AIN'T NOBODY TOOK CARE OF ME UP IN BALTIMORE.

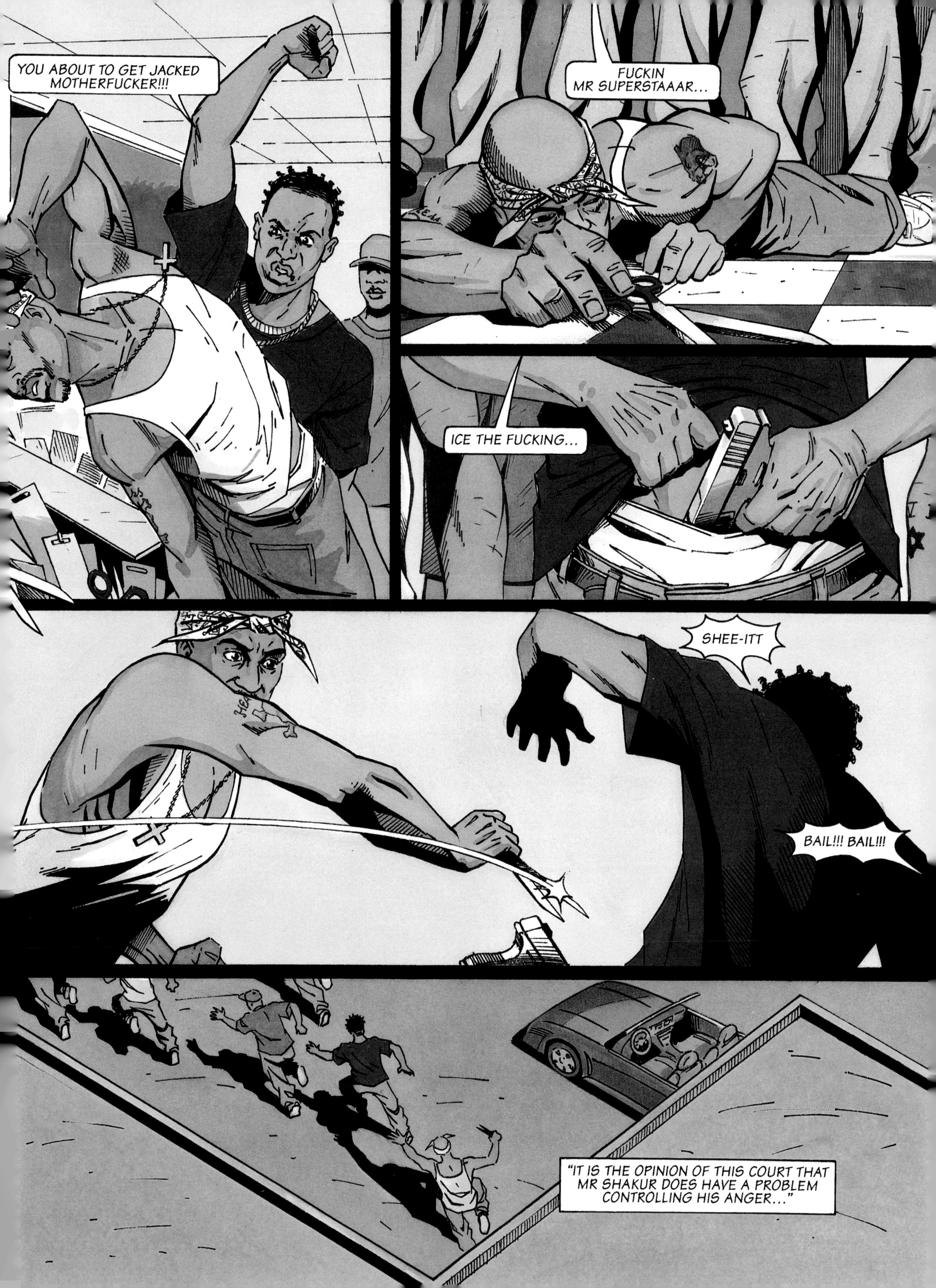
YOU ABOUT TO GET JACKED MOTHERFUCKER!!!
FUCKIN MR SUPERSTAAAR...
ICE THE FUCKING...
SHEE-ITT
BAIL!!! BAIL!!!
"IT IS THE OPINION OF THIS COURT THAT MR SHAKUR DOES HAVE A PROBLEM CONTROLLING HIS ANGER..."

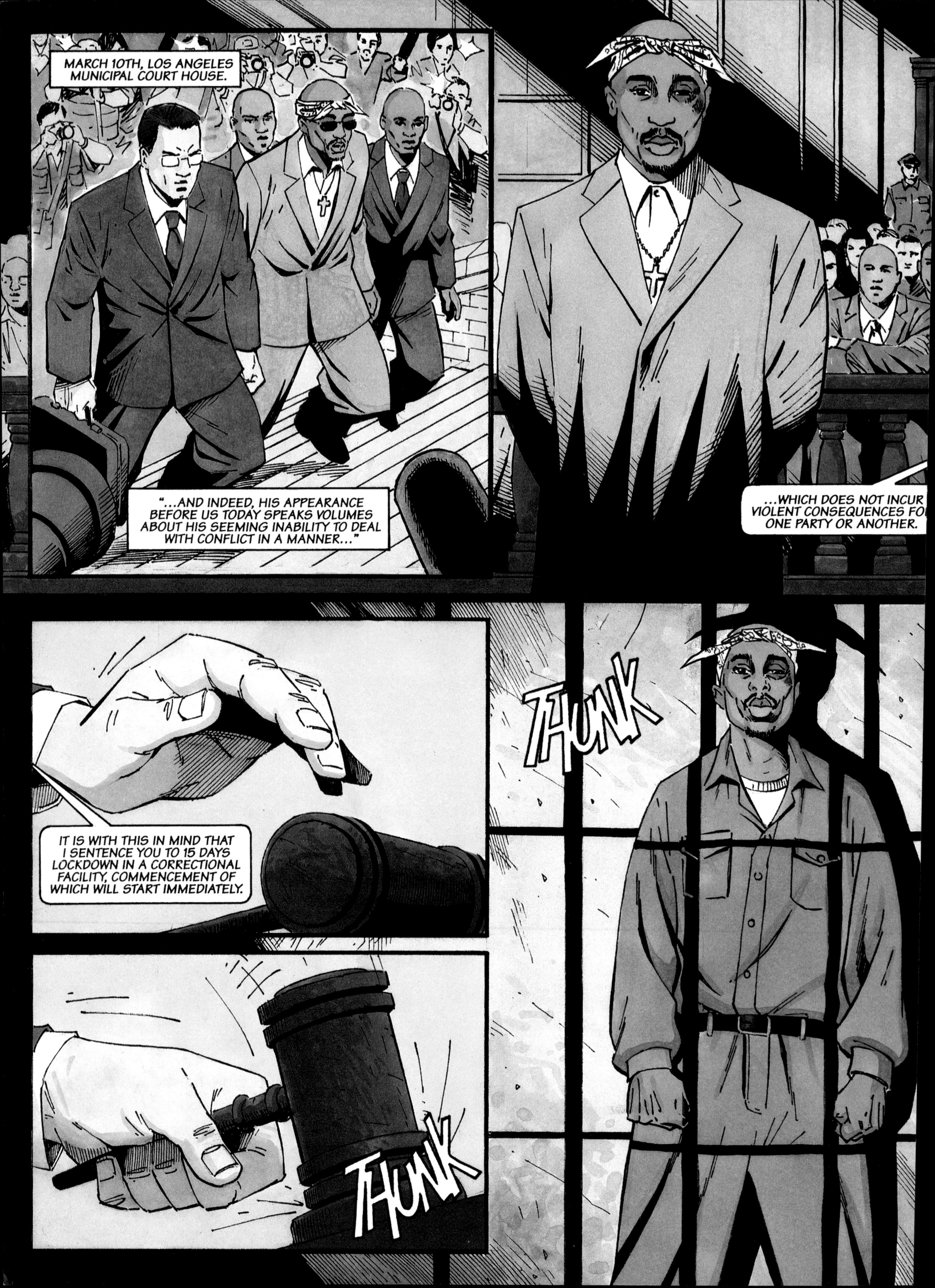
MARCH 10TH, LOS ANGELES MUNICIPAL COURT HOUSE.
"...AND INDEED, HIS APPEARANCE BEFORE US TODAY SPEAKS VOLUMES ABOUT HIS SEEMING INABILITY TO DEAL WITH CONFLICT IN A MANNER..."
...WHICH DOES NOT INCUR VIOLENT CONSEQUENCES FO ONE PARTY OR ANOTHER.
IT IS WITH THIS IN MIND THAT I SENTENCE YOU TO 15 DAYS LOCKDOWN IN A CORRECTIONAL FACILITY, COMMENCEMENT OF WHICH WILL START IMMEDIATELY.
THUNK
THUNK

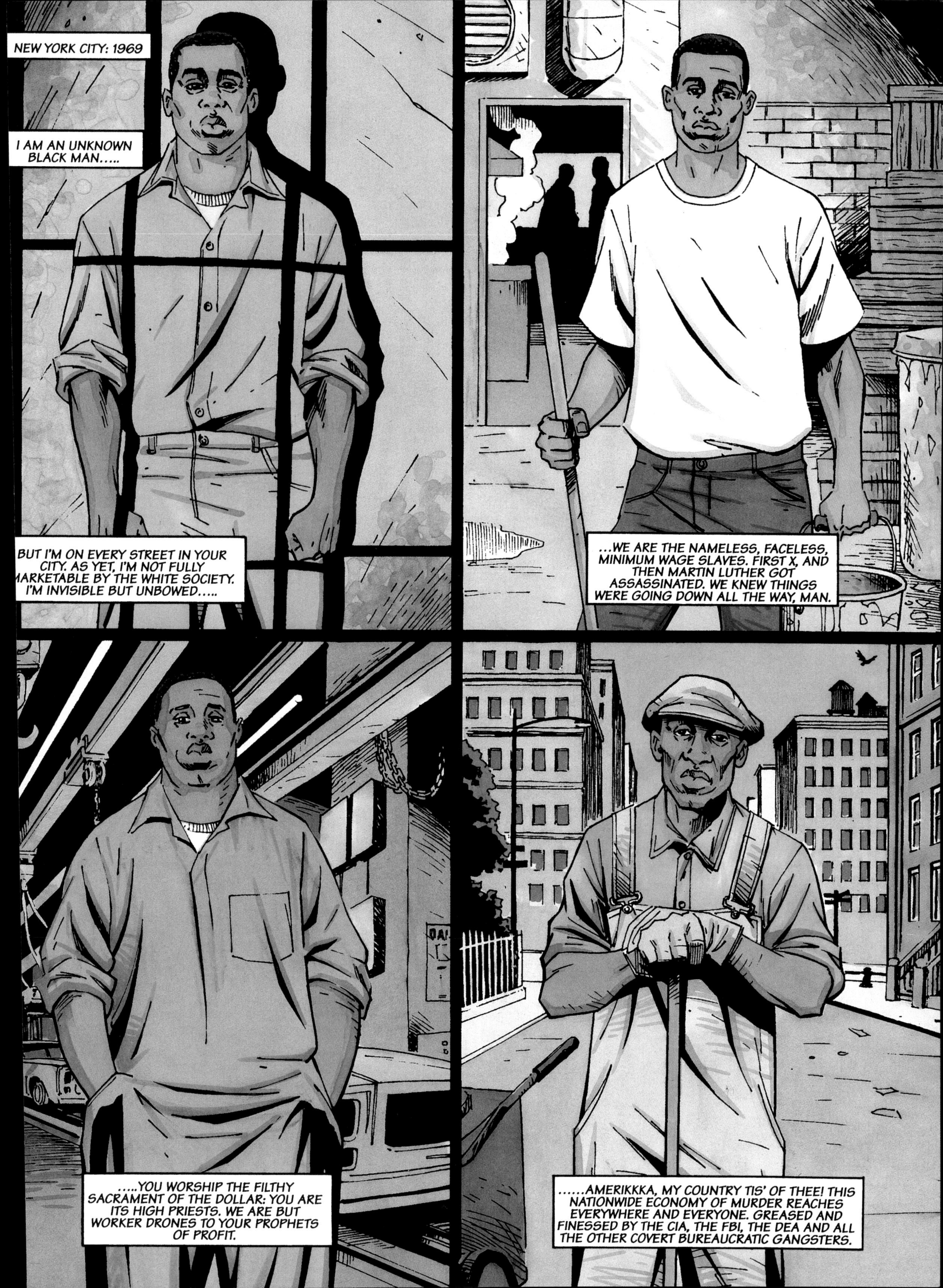
NEW YORK CITY: 1969
I AM AN UNKNOWN BLACK MAN…..
BUT I'M ON EVERY STREET IN YOUR CITY. AS YET, I'M NOT FULLY MARKETABLE BY THE WHITE SOCIETY. I'M INVISIBLE BUT UNBOWED…..
…WE ARE THE NAMELESS, FACELESS, MINIMUM WAGE SLAVES. FIRST X, AND THEN MARTIN LUTHER GOT ASSASSINATED. WE KNEW THINGS WERE GOING DOWN ALL THE WAY, MAN.
…..YOU WORSHIP THE FILTHY SACRAMENT OF THE DOLLAR: YOU ARE ITS HIGH PRIESTS. WE ARE BUT WORKER DRONES TO YOUR PROPHETS OF PROFIT.
……AMERIKKKA, MY COUNTRY TIS' OF THEE! THIS NATIONWIDE ECONOMY OF MURDER REACHES EVERYWHERE AND EVERYONE. GREASED AND FINESSED BY THE CIA, THE FBI, THE DEA AND ALL THE OTHER COVERT BUREAUCRATIC GANGSTERS.

THIS IS YOUR SOUL SISTER UP IN HERE... THINGS ARE GOING TO BE HOTTIN' UP HERE STATESIDE, DRUGS JUST BE POURING AL' A TIME INTO MY GHETTOES......

...COVERT OPERATIONS INFILTRATE THE CIVIL RIGHTS MOVEMENTS.........

I WANT TO INVESTIGATE THIS BLACK PANTHER PARTY AND PLA INFILTRATORS THAT WILL SOW MISTRUST AND SEDITION IN THE RANKS. GOD BLESS AMERICA.

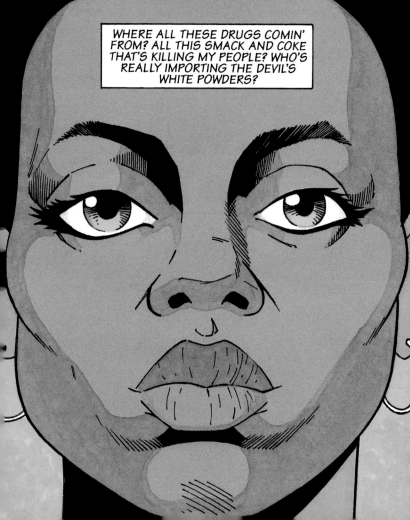

WHERE ALL THESE DRUGS COMIN' FROM? ALL THIS SMACK AND COKE THAT'S KILLING MY PEOPLE? WHO'S REALLY IMPORTING THE DEVIL'S WHITE POWDERS?

SEPTEMBER 8, 1968: FBI HQ, WASHINGTON DC

I CONSIDER THE BLACK PANTHERS TO BE THE SINGLE GREATEST THREAT TO THE INTERNAL SECURITY OF THIS GREAT COUNTRY OF OURS.

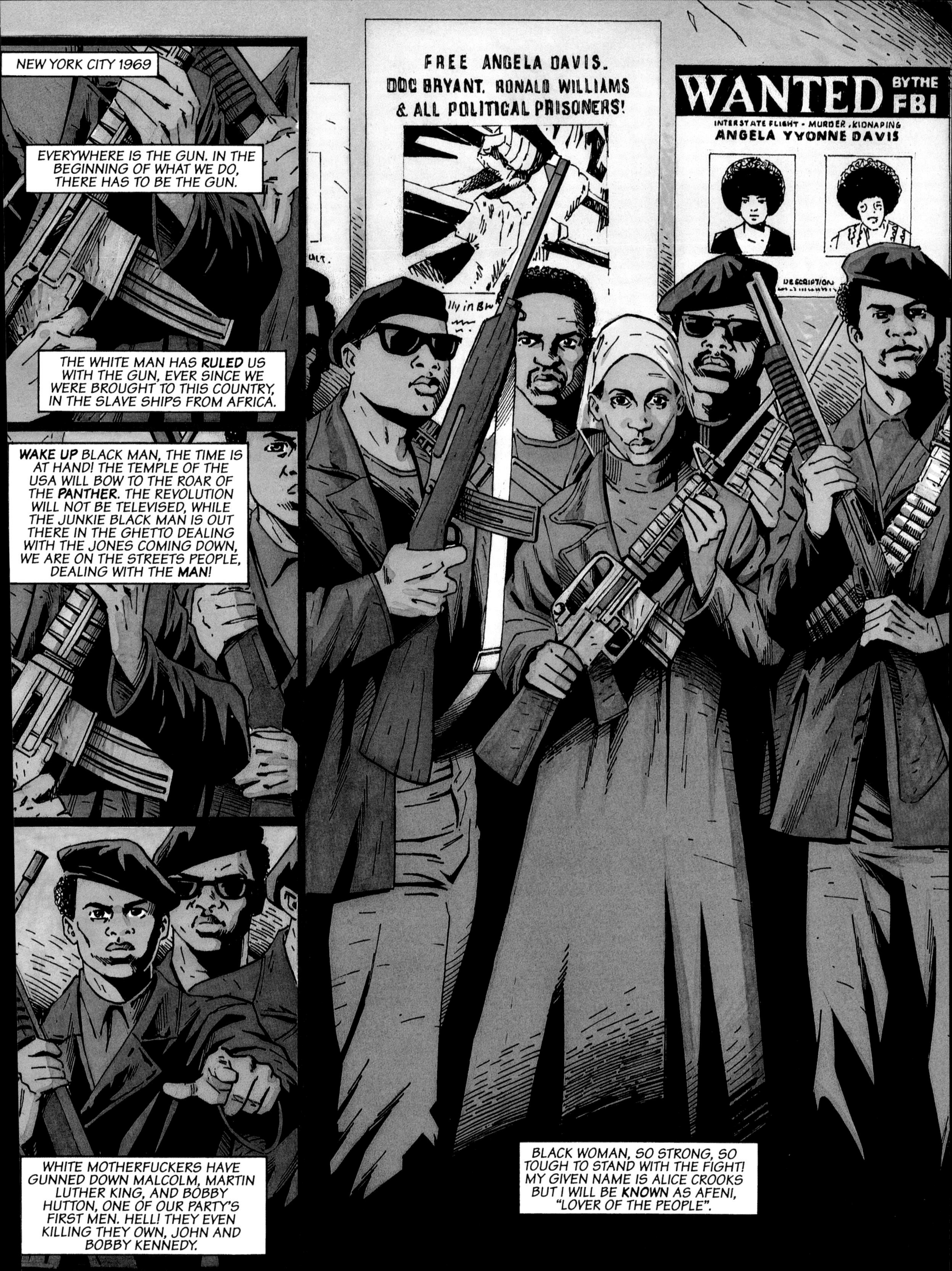

NEW YORK CITY 1969
EVERYWHERE IS THE GUN. IN THE BEGINNING OF WHAT WE DO, THERE HAS TO BE THE GUN.
THE WHITE MAN HAS **RULED** US WITH THE GUN, EVER SINCE WE WERE BROUGHT TO THIS COUNTRY, IN THE SLAVE SHIPS FROM AFRICA.
WAKE UP BLACK MAN, THE TIME IS AT HAND! THE TEMPLE OF THE USA WILL BOW TO THE ROAR OF THE **PANTHER**. THE REVOLUTION WILL NOT BE TELEVISED, WHILE THE JUNKIE BLACK MAN IS OUT THERE IN THE GHETTO DEALING WITH THE JONES COMING DOWN, WE ARE ON THE STREETS PEOPLE, DEALING WITH THE **MAN**!
WHITE MOTHERFUCKERS HAVE GUNNED DOWN MALCOLM, MARTIN LUTHER KING, AND BOBBY HUTTON, ONE OF OUR PARTY'S FIRST MEN. HELL! THEY EVEN KILLING THEY OWN, JOHN AND BOBBY KENNEDY.
FREE ANGELA DAVIS. DOC BRYANT. RONALD WILLIAMS & ALL POLITICAL PRISONERS!
WANTED BY THE FBI
INTERSTATE FLIGHT - MURDER, KIDNAPING
ANGELA YYONNE DAVIS
DESCRIPTION
BLACK WOMAN, SO STRONG, SO TOUGH TO STAND WITH THE FIGHT! MY GIVEN NAME IS ALICE CROOKS BUT I WILL BE **KNOWN** AS AFENI, "LOVER OF THE PEOPLE".

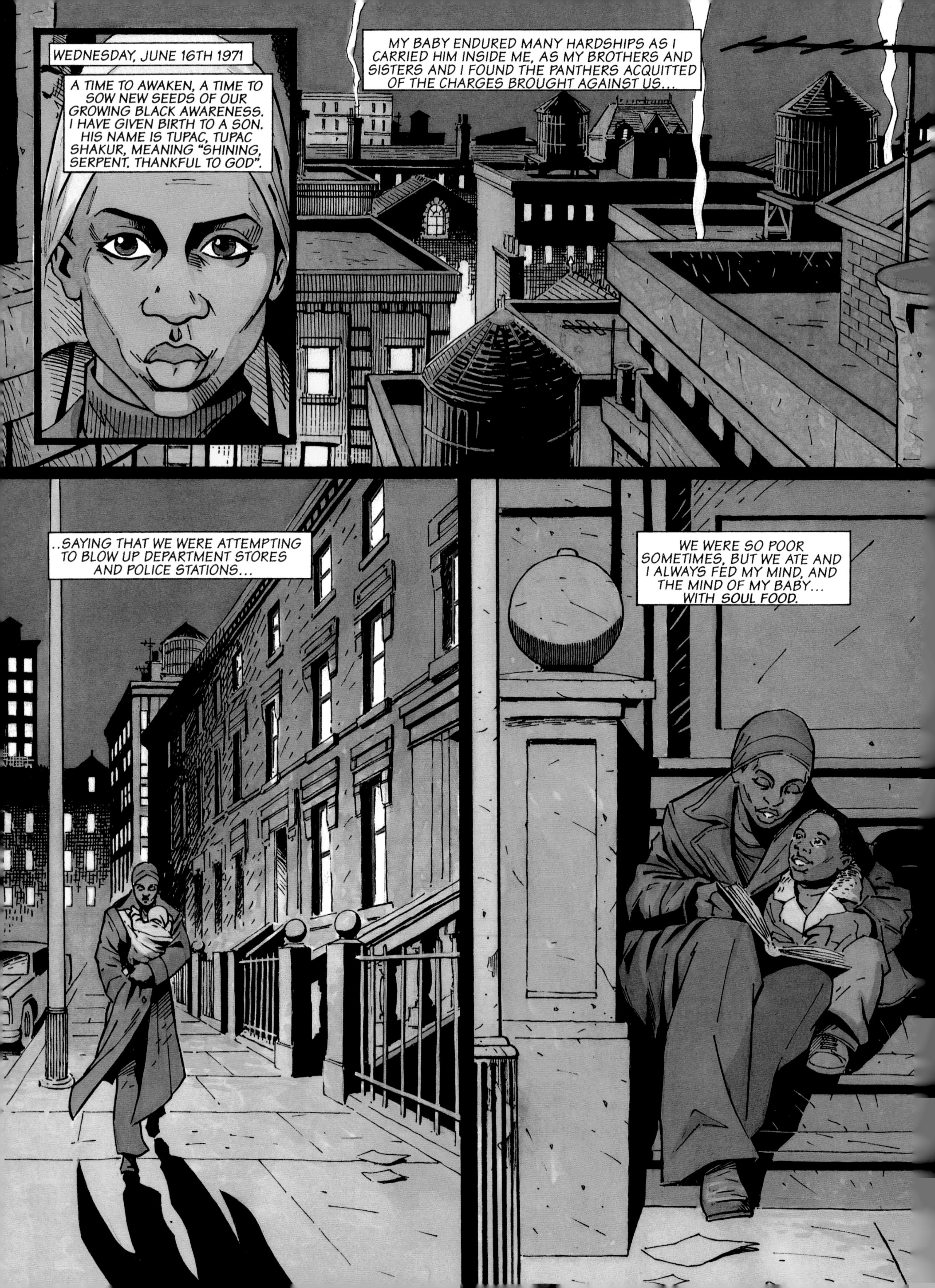
WEDNESDAY, JUNE 16TH 1971
A TIME TO AWAKEN, A TIME TO SOW NEW SEEDS OF OUR GROWING BLACK AWARENESS. I HAVE GIVEN BIRTH TO A SON. HIS NAME IS TUPAC, TUPAC SHAKUR, MEANING "SHINING, SERPENT, THANKFUL TO GOD".
MY BABY ENDURED MANY HARDSHIPS AS I CARRIED HIM INSIDE ME, AS MY BROTHERS AND SISTERS AND I FOUND THE PANTHERS ACQUITTED OF THE CHARGES BROUGHT AGAINST US...
..SAYING THAT WE WERE ATTEMPTING TO BLOW UP DEPARTMENT STORES AND POLICE STATIONS...
WE WERE SO POOR SOMETIMES, BUT WE ATE AND I ALWAYS FED MY MIND, AND THE MIND OF MY BABY... WITH SOUL FOOD.

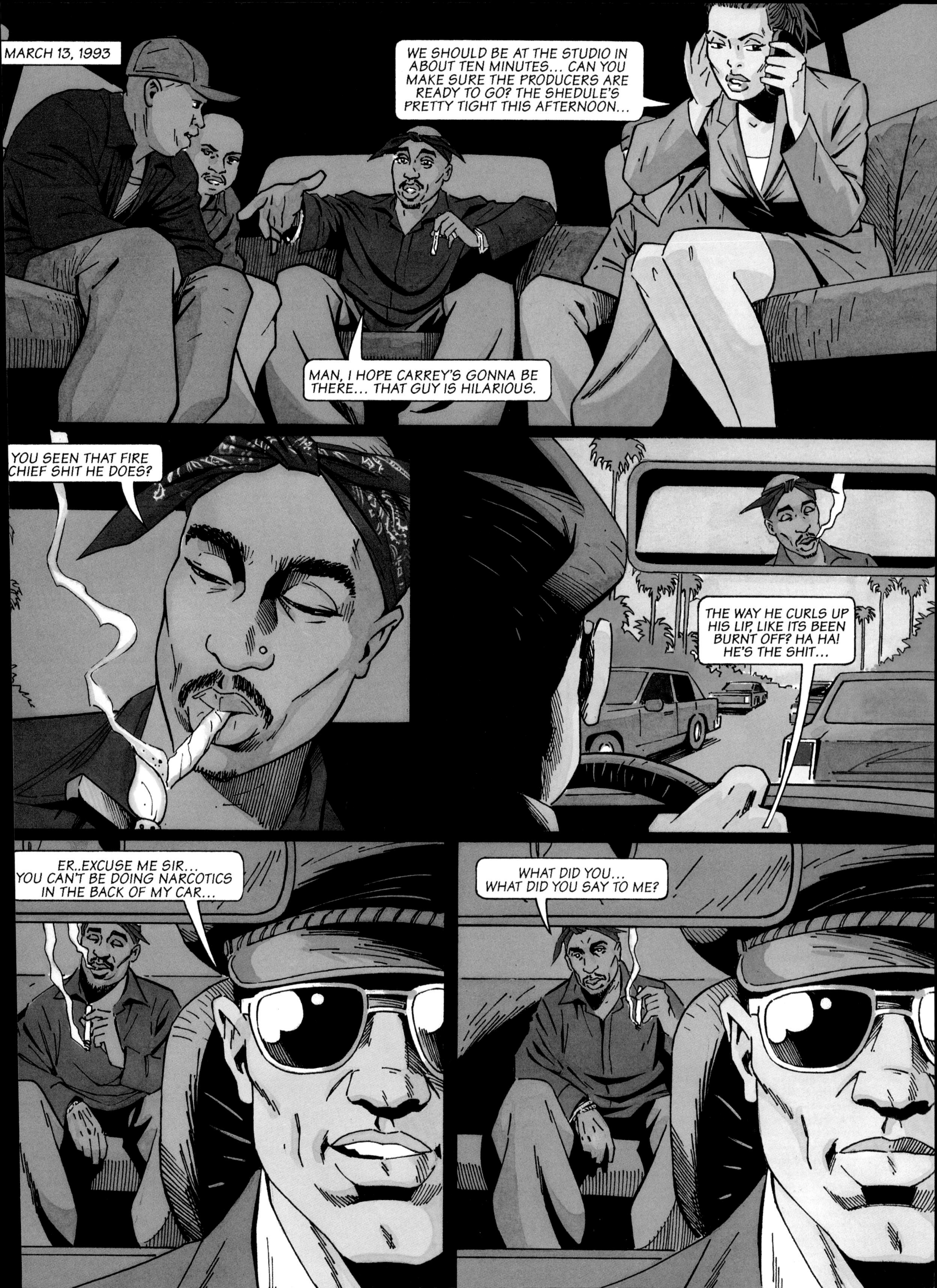
MARCH 13, 1993
WE SHOULD BE AT THE STUDIO IN ABOUT TEN MINUTES... CAN YOU MAKE SURE THE PRODUCERS ARE READY TO GO? THE SHEDULE'S PRETTY TIGHT THIS AFTERNOON...
MAN, I HOPE CARREY'S GONNA BE THERE... THAT GUY IS HILARIOUS.
YOU SEEN THAT FIRE CHIEF SHIT HE DOES?
THE WAY HE CURLS UP HIS LIP, LIKE ITS BEEN BURNT OFF? HA HA! HE'S THE SHIT...
ER..EXCUSE ME SIR... YOU CAN'T BE DOING NARCOTICS IN THE BACK OF MY CAR...
WHAT DID YOU... WHAT DID YOU SAY TO ME?

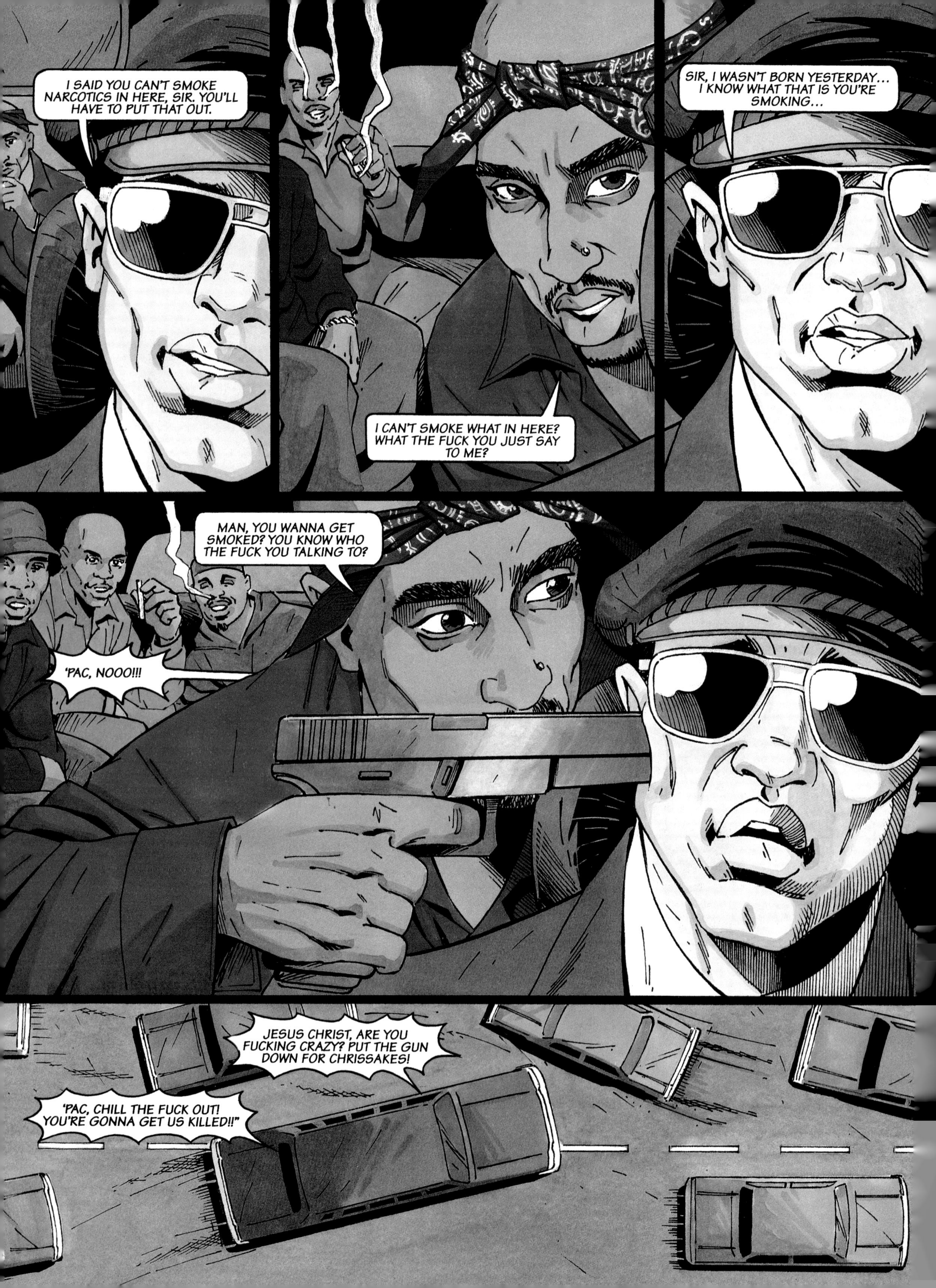
I SAID YOU CAN'T SMOKE NARCOTICS IN HERE, SIR. YOU'LL HAVE TO PUT THAT OUT.
I CAN'T SMOKE WHAT IN HERE? WHAT THE FUCK YOU JUST SAY TO ME?
SIR, I WASN'T BORN YESTERDAY… I KNOW WHAT THAT IS YOU'RE SMOKING…
MAN, YOU WANNA GET SMOKED? YOU KNOW WHO THE FUCK YOU TALKING TO?
'PAC, NOOO!!!
JESUS CHRIST, ARE YOU FUCKING CRAZY? PUT THE GUN DOWN FOR CHRISSAKES!
'PAC, CHILL THE FUCK OUT! YOU'RE GONNA GET US KILLED!!"

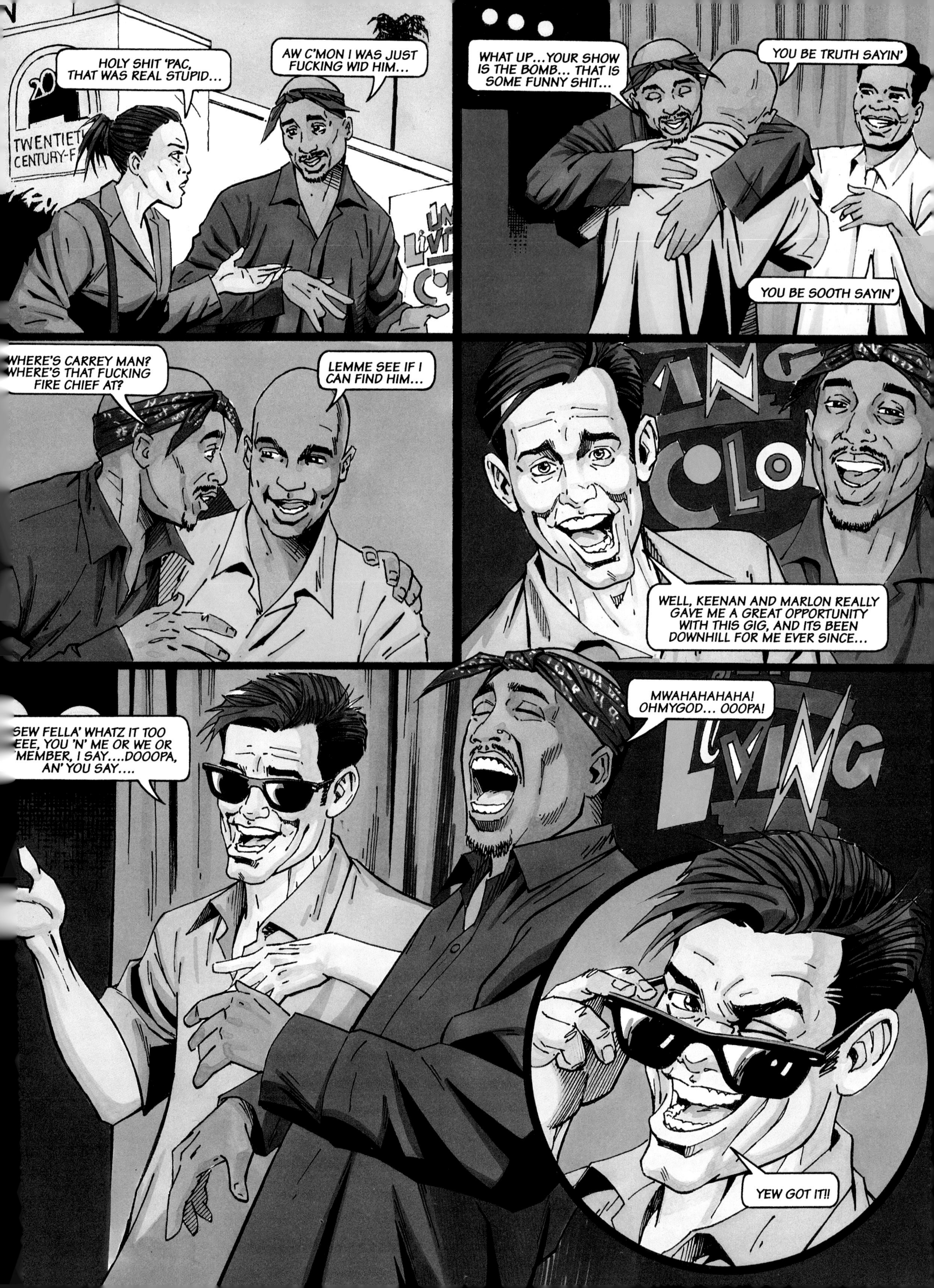
HOLY SHIT 'PAC, THAT WAS REAL STUPID...
AW C'MON I WAS JUST FUCKING WID HIM...
TWENTIETH CENTURY-F
WHAT UP...YOUR SHOW IS THE BOMB... THAT IS SOME FUNNY SHIT...
YOU BE TRUTH SAYIN'
YOU BE SOOTH SAYIN'
WHERE'S CARREY MAN? WHERE'S THAT FUCKING FIRE CHIEF AT?
LEMME SEE IF I CAN FIND HIM...
WELL, KEENAN AND MARLON REALLY GAVE ME A GREAT OPPORTUNITY WITH THIS GIG, AND ITS BEEN DOWNHILL FOR ME EVER SINCE...
SEW FELLA' WHATZ IT TOO EEE, YOU 'N' ME OR WE OR 'MEMBER, I SAY....DOOOPA, AN' YOU SAY....
MWAHAHAHAHA! OHMYGOD... OOOPA!
YEW GOT IT!!

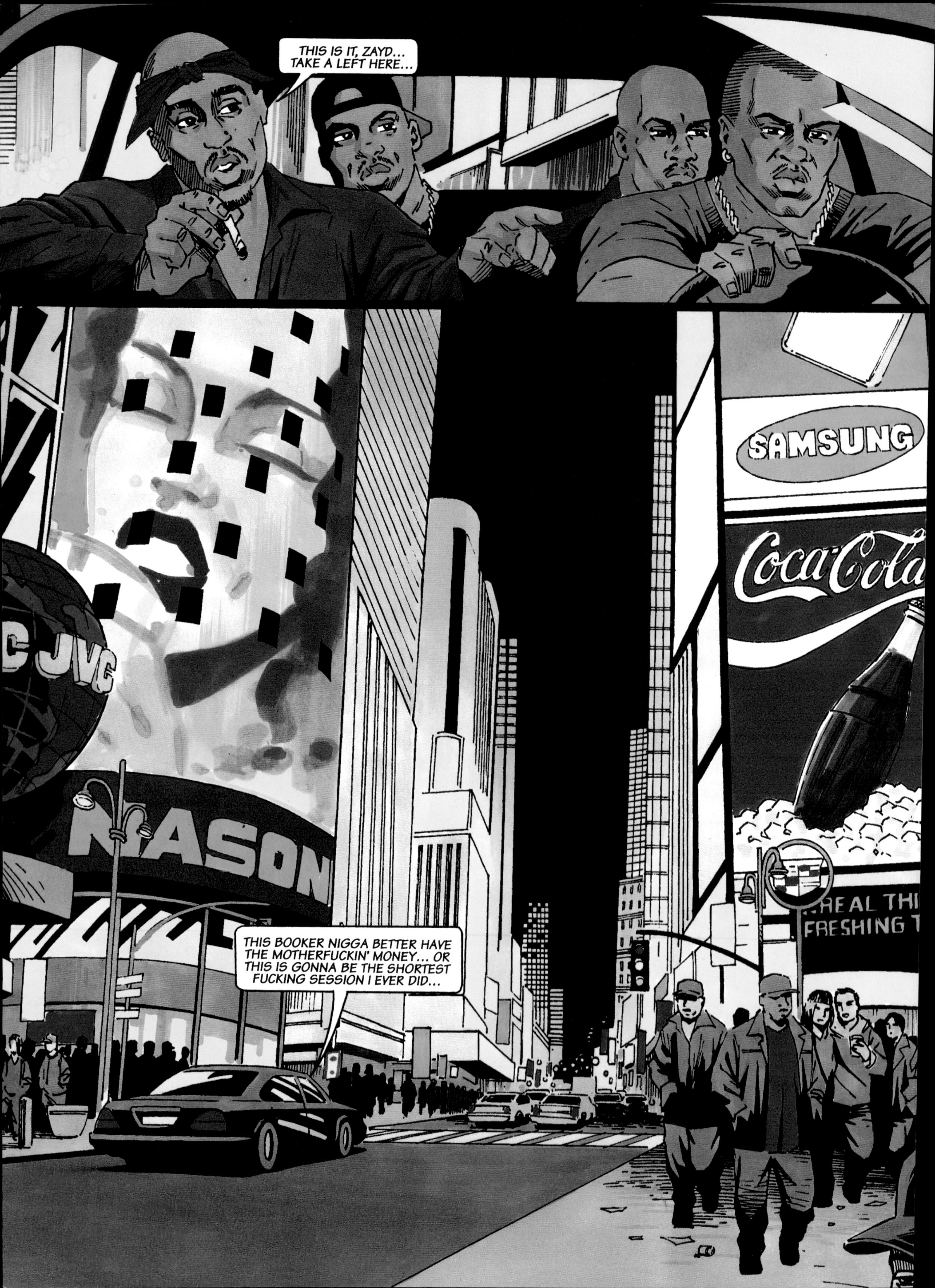
THIS IS IT, ZAYD... TAKE A LEFT HERE...
SAMSUNG
Coca-Cola
JVC
THIS BOOKER NIGGA BETTER HAVE THE MOTHERFUCKIN' MONEY... OR THIS IS GONNA BE THE SHORTEST FUCKING SESSION I EVER DID...

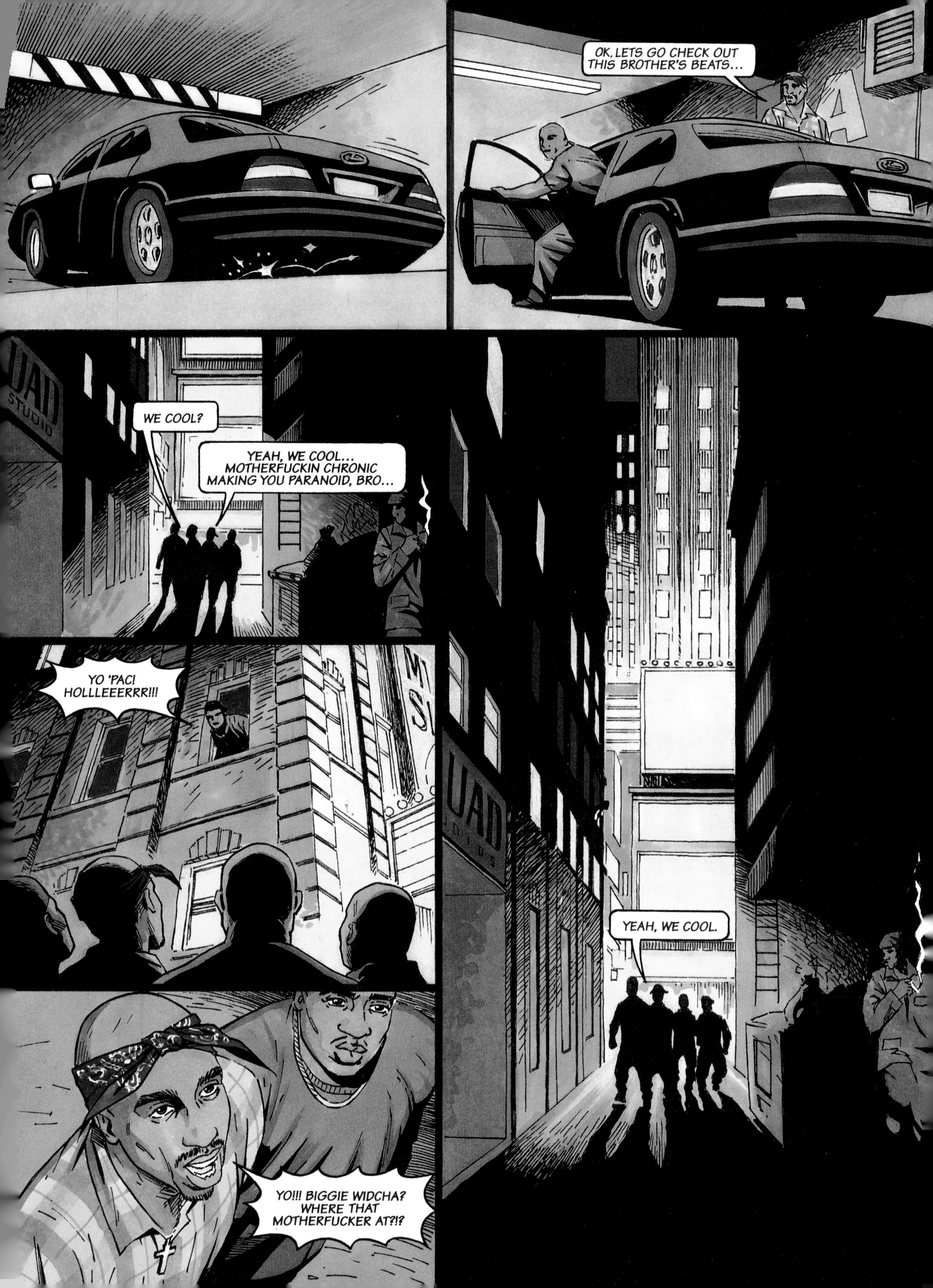
OK, LETS GO CHECK OUT THIS BROTHER'S BEATS...
STUDIO
WE COOL?
YEAH, WE COOL... MOTHERFUCKIN CHRONIC MAKING YOU PARANOID, BRO...
YO 'PAC! HOLLLEEERRR!!!
YO!!! BIGGIE WIDCHA? WHERE THAT MOTHERFUCKER AT?!?
YEAH, WE COOL.

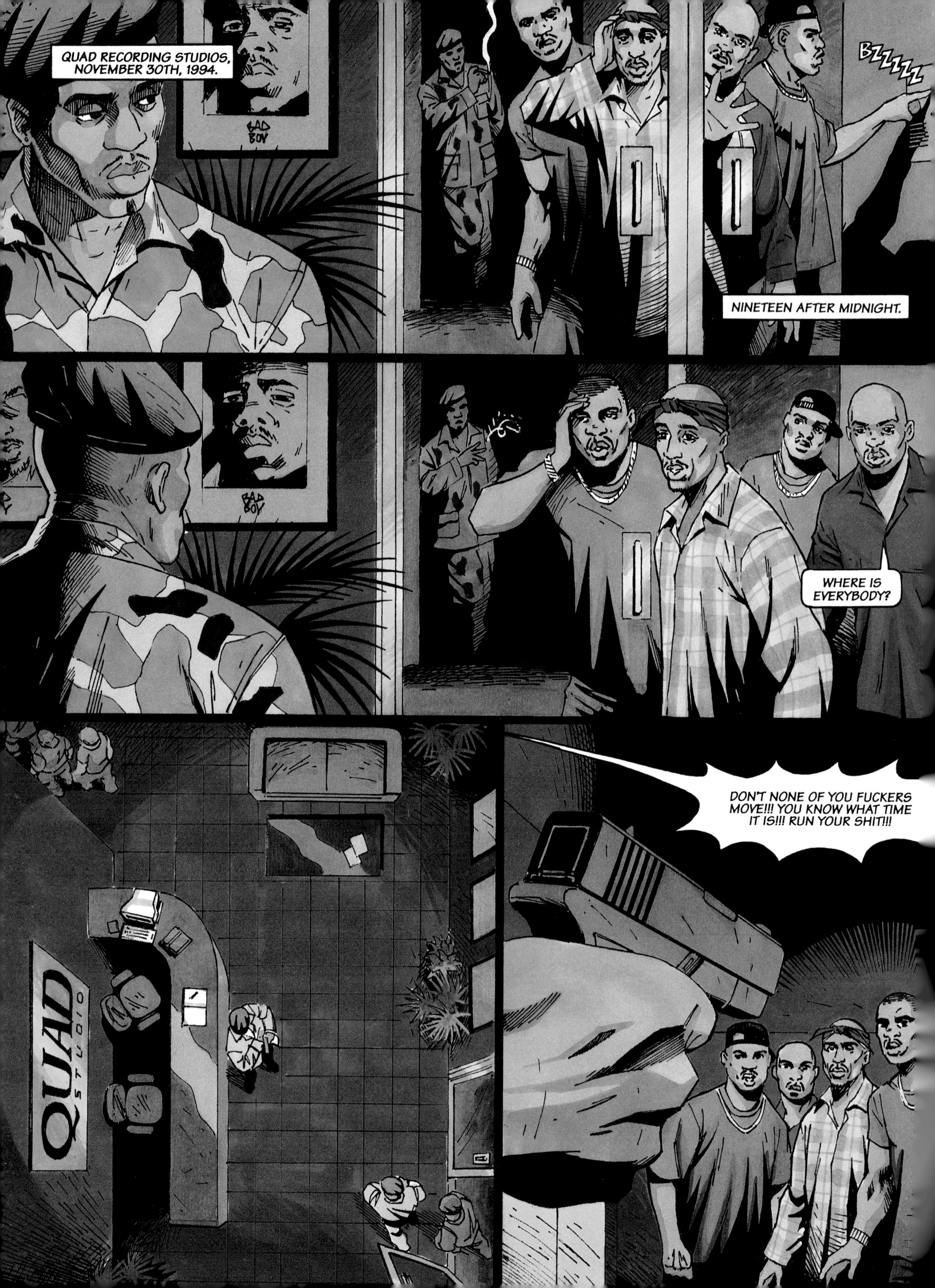
QUAD RECORDING STUDIOS, NOVEMBER 30TH, 1994.
BAD BOY
BZZZZZZ
NINETEEN AFTER MIDNIGHT.
BAD BOY
WHERE IS EVERYBODY?
QUAD STUDIO
DON'T NONE OF YOU FUCKERS MOVE!!! YOU KNOW WHAT TIME IT IS!!! RUN YOUR SHIT!!!

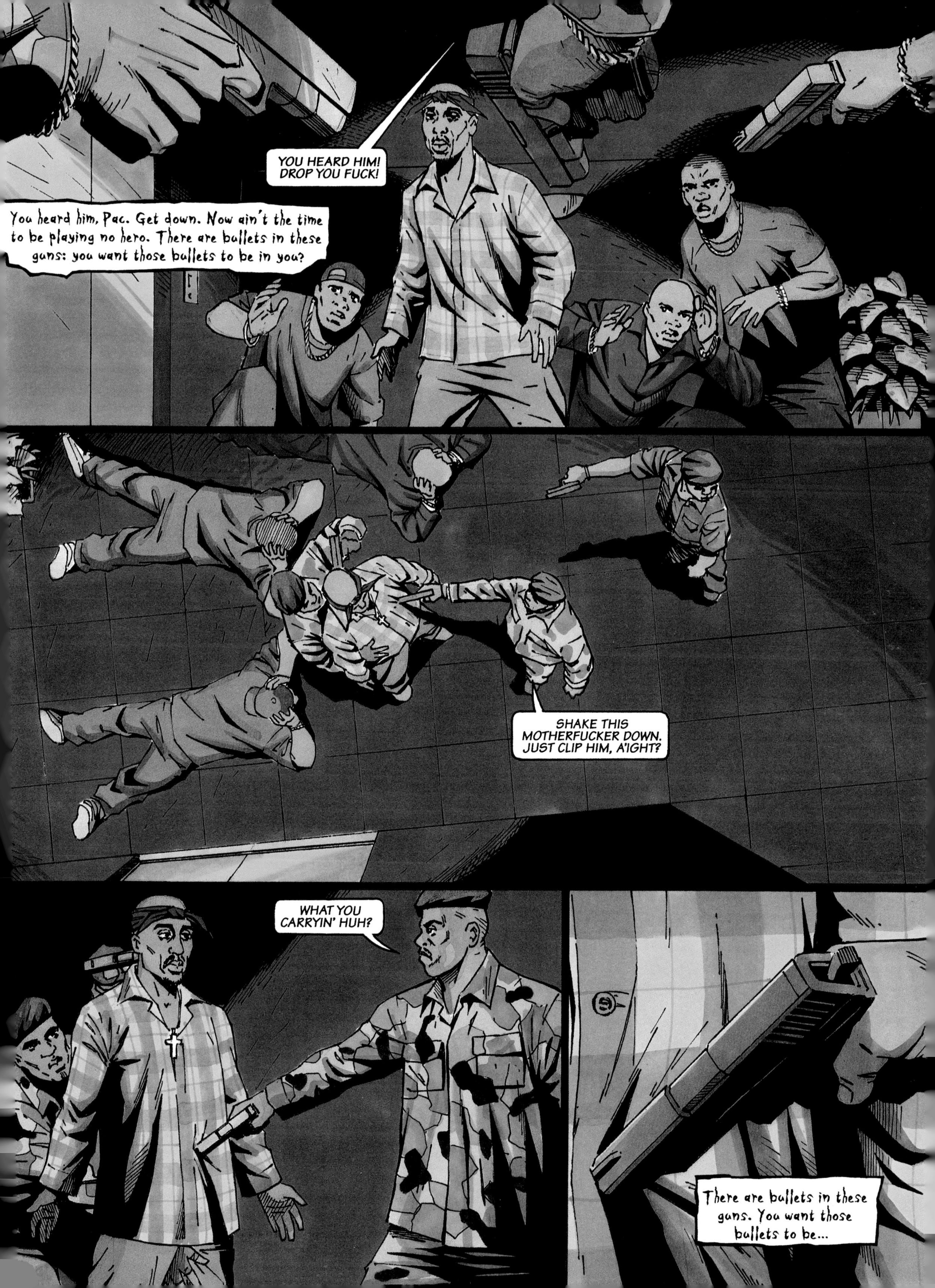
You heard him, Pac. Get down. Now ain't the time to be playing no hero. There are bullets in these guns: you want those bullets to be in you?
YOU HEARD HIM! DROP YOU FUCK!
SHAKE THIS MOTHERFUCKER DOWN. JUST CLIP HIM, A'IGHT?
WHAT YOU CARRYIN' HUH?
There are bullets in these guns. You want those bullets to be...

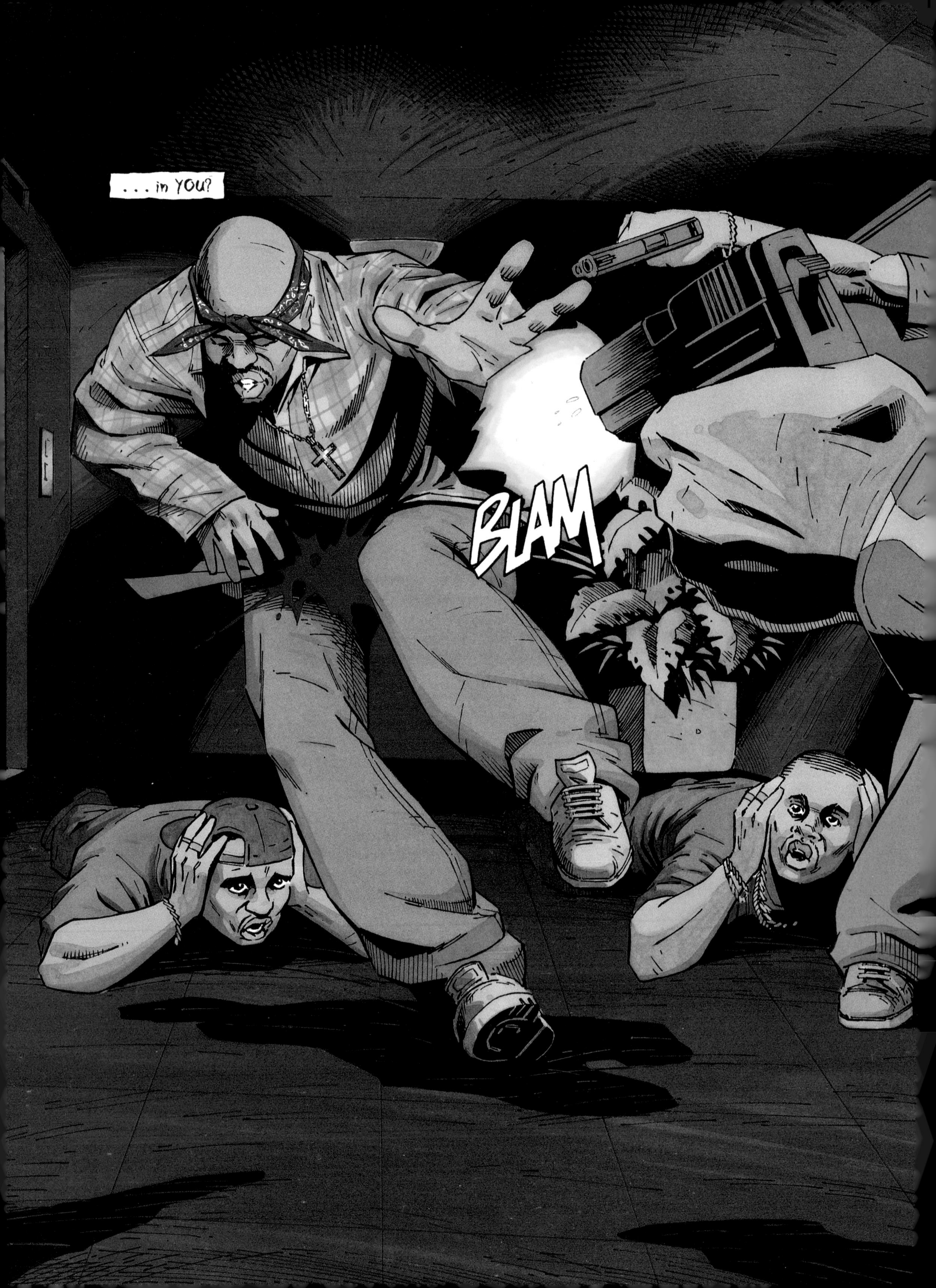
. . . in YOU?
BLAM

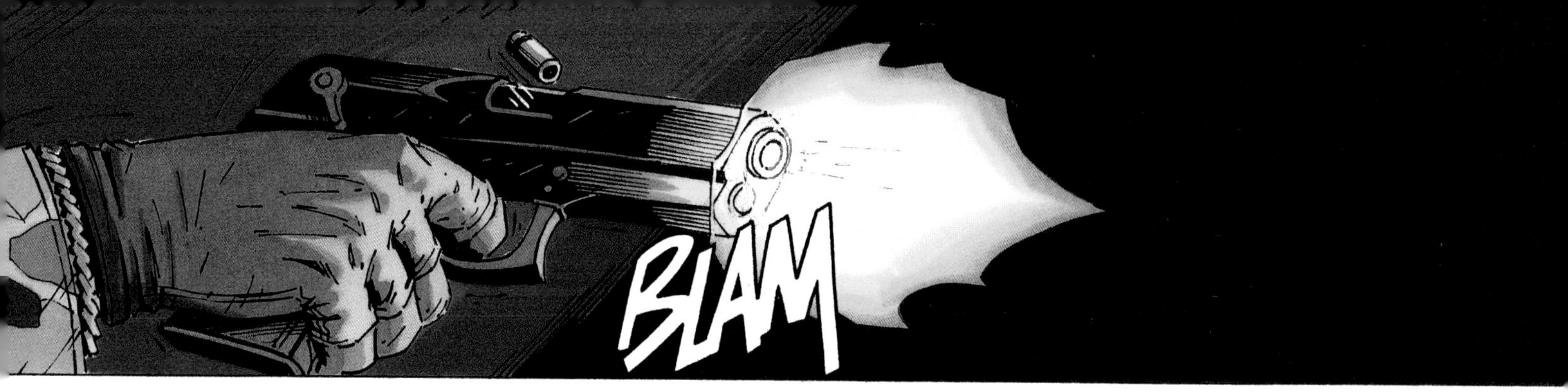
BLAM

NINE MILLIMETRES.

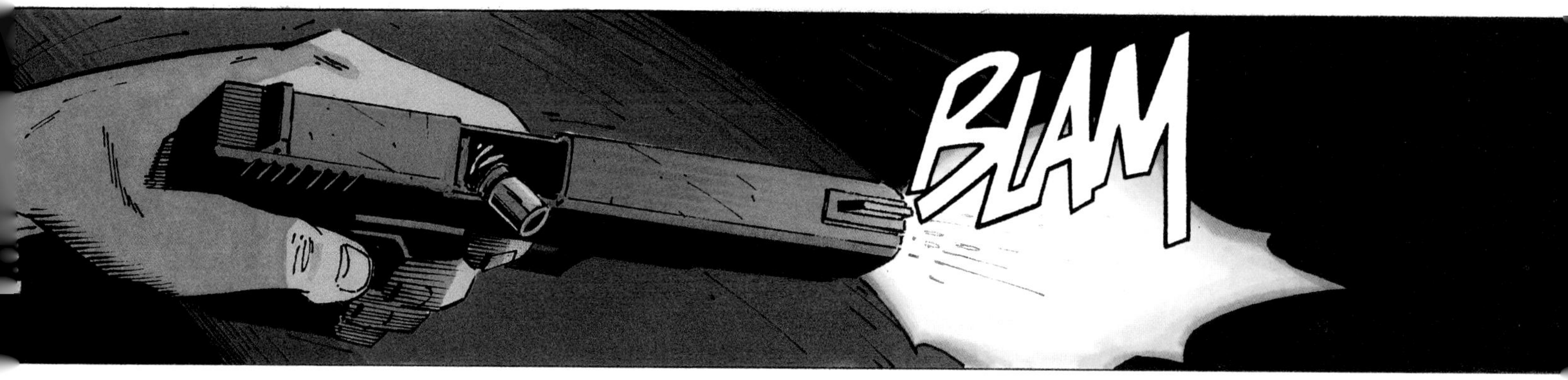
BLAM

NINE MILLMETRES JUST KEEPS COMING.

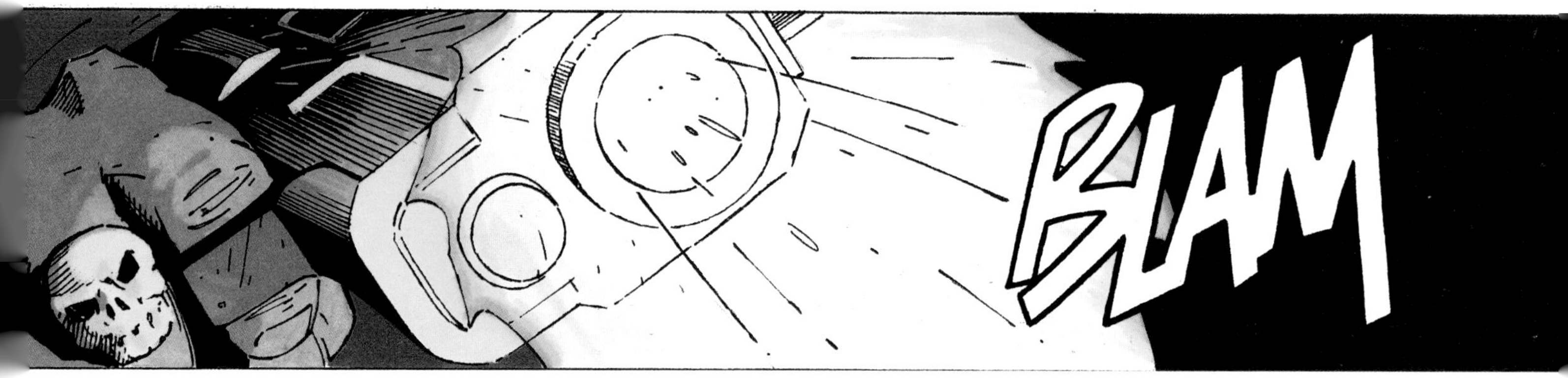
BLAM

SHIT GETS HAZY.

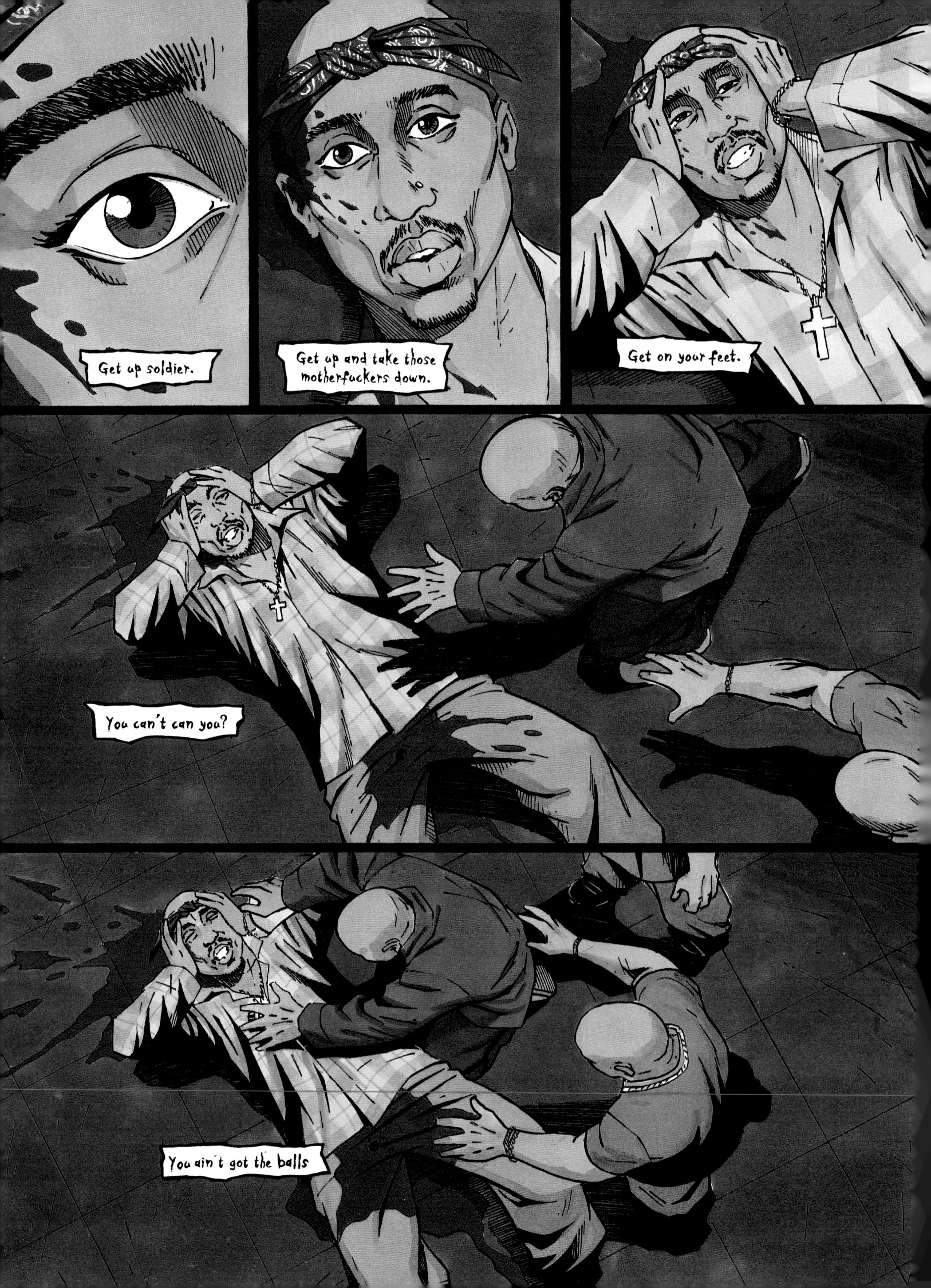

Get up soldier.
Get up and take those motherfuckers down.
Get on your feet.
You can't can you?
You ain't got the balls

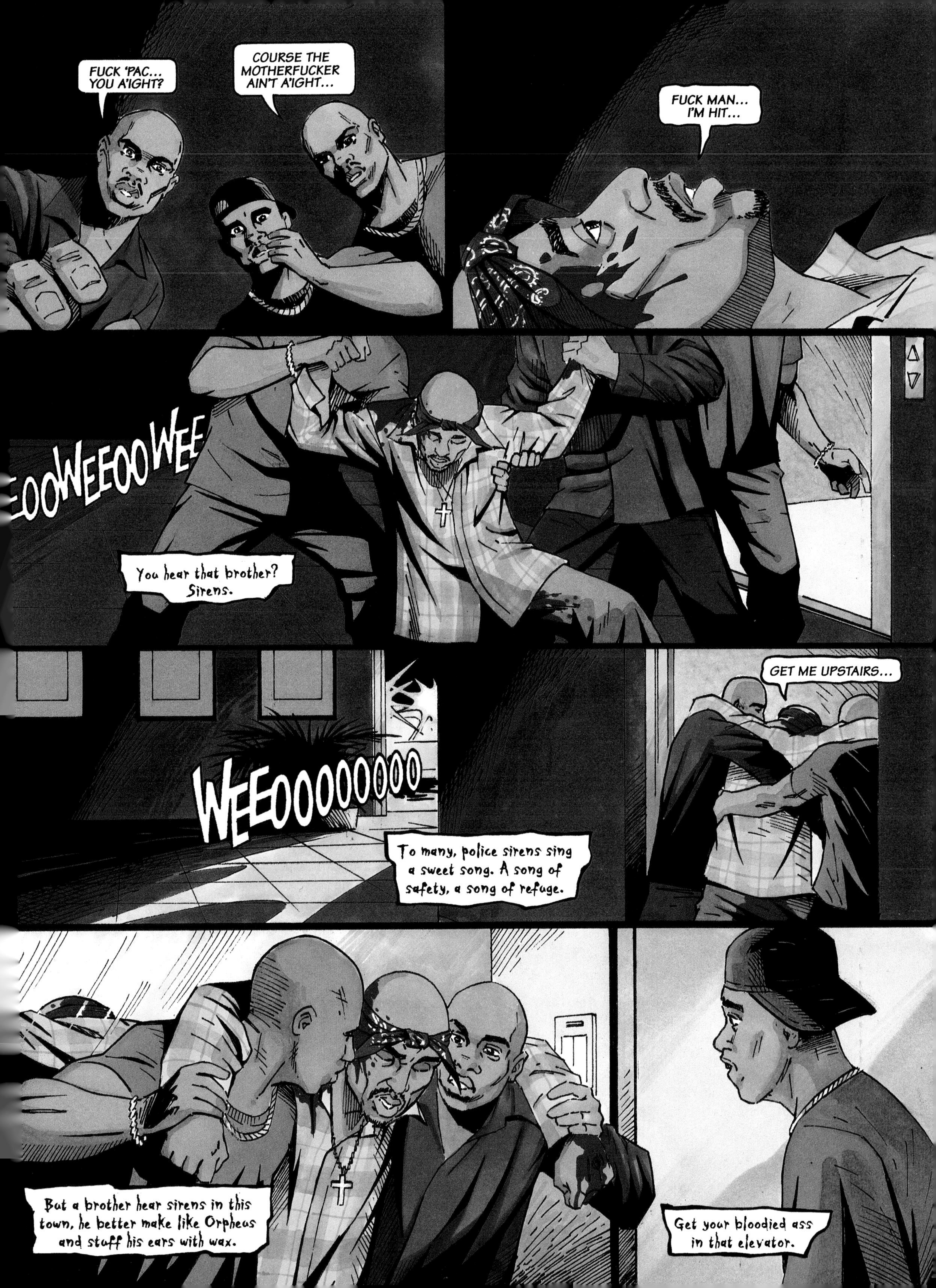
FUCK 'PAC... YOU A'IGHT?
COURSE THE MOTHERFUCKER AIN'T A'IGHT...
FUCK MAN... I'M HIT...
EOOWEEOOWEE
You hear that brother? Sirens.
WEEOOOOOOOO
To many, police sirens sing a sweet song. A song of safety, a song of refuge.
GET ME UPSTAIRS...
But a brother hear sirens in this town, he better make like Orpheus and stuff his ears with wax.
Get your bloodied ass in that elevator.

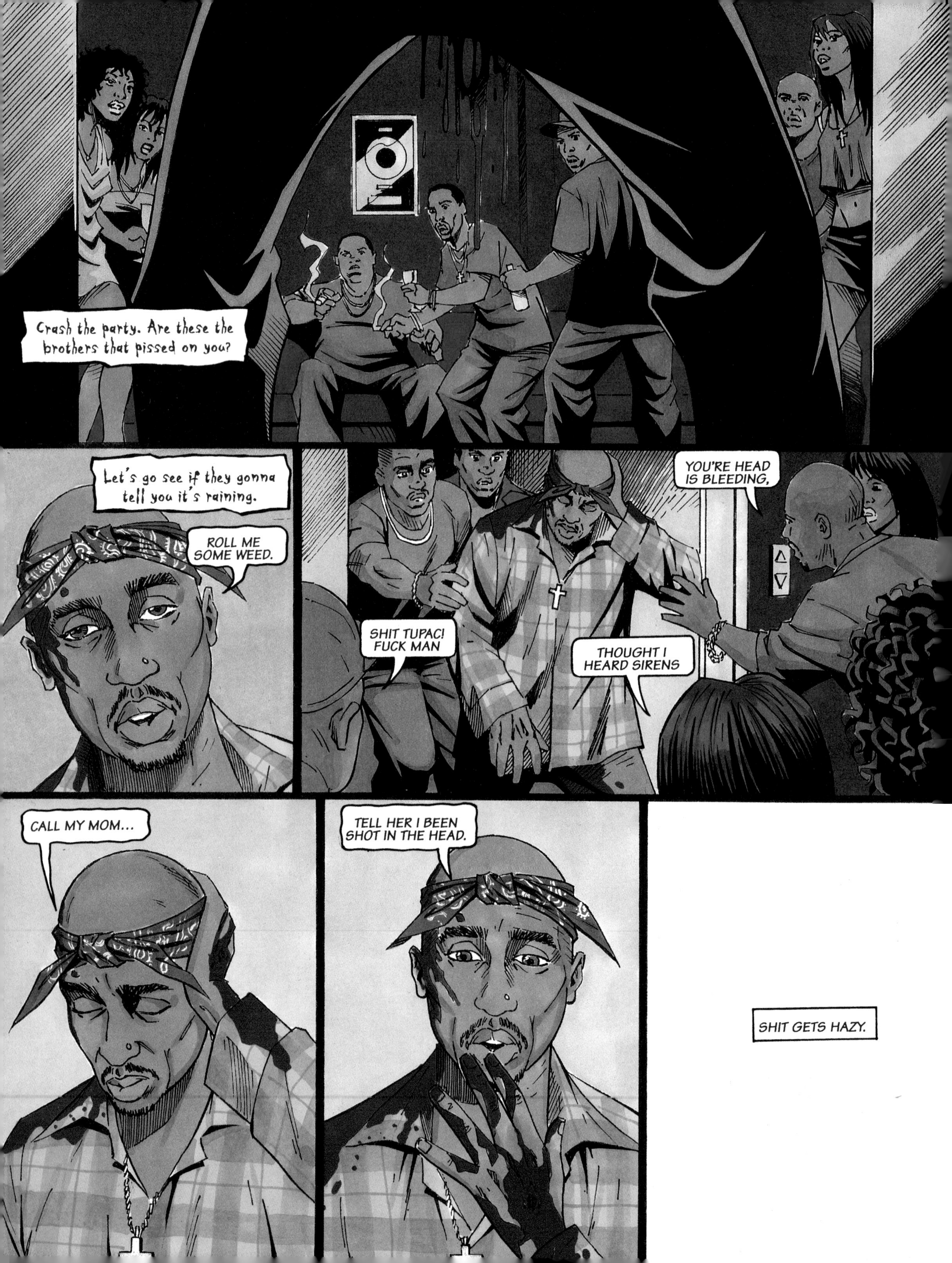
Crash the party. Are these the brothers that pissed on you?
Let's go see if they gonna tell you it's raining.
ROLL ME SOME WEED.
YOU'RE HEAD IS BLEEDING,
SHIT TUPAC! FUCK MAN
THOUGHT I HEARD SIRENS
CALL MY MOM...
TELL HER I BEEN SHOT IN THE HEAD.
SHIT GETS HAZY.

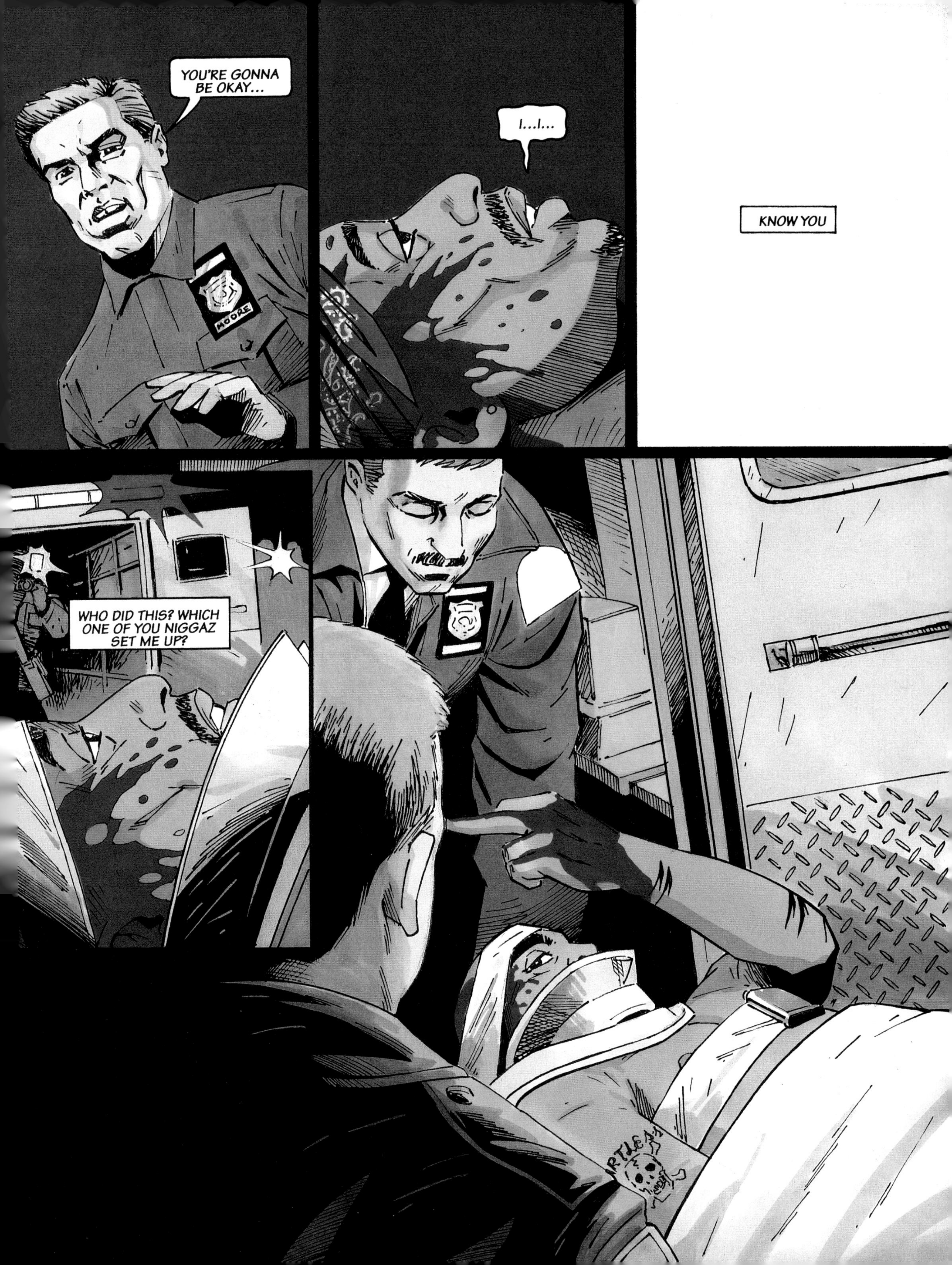
YOU'RE GONNA BE OKAY...
MOORE
I...I...
KNOW YOU
WHO DID THIS? WHICH ONE OF YOU NIGGAZ SET ME UP?

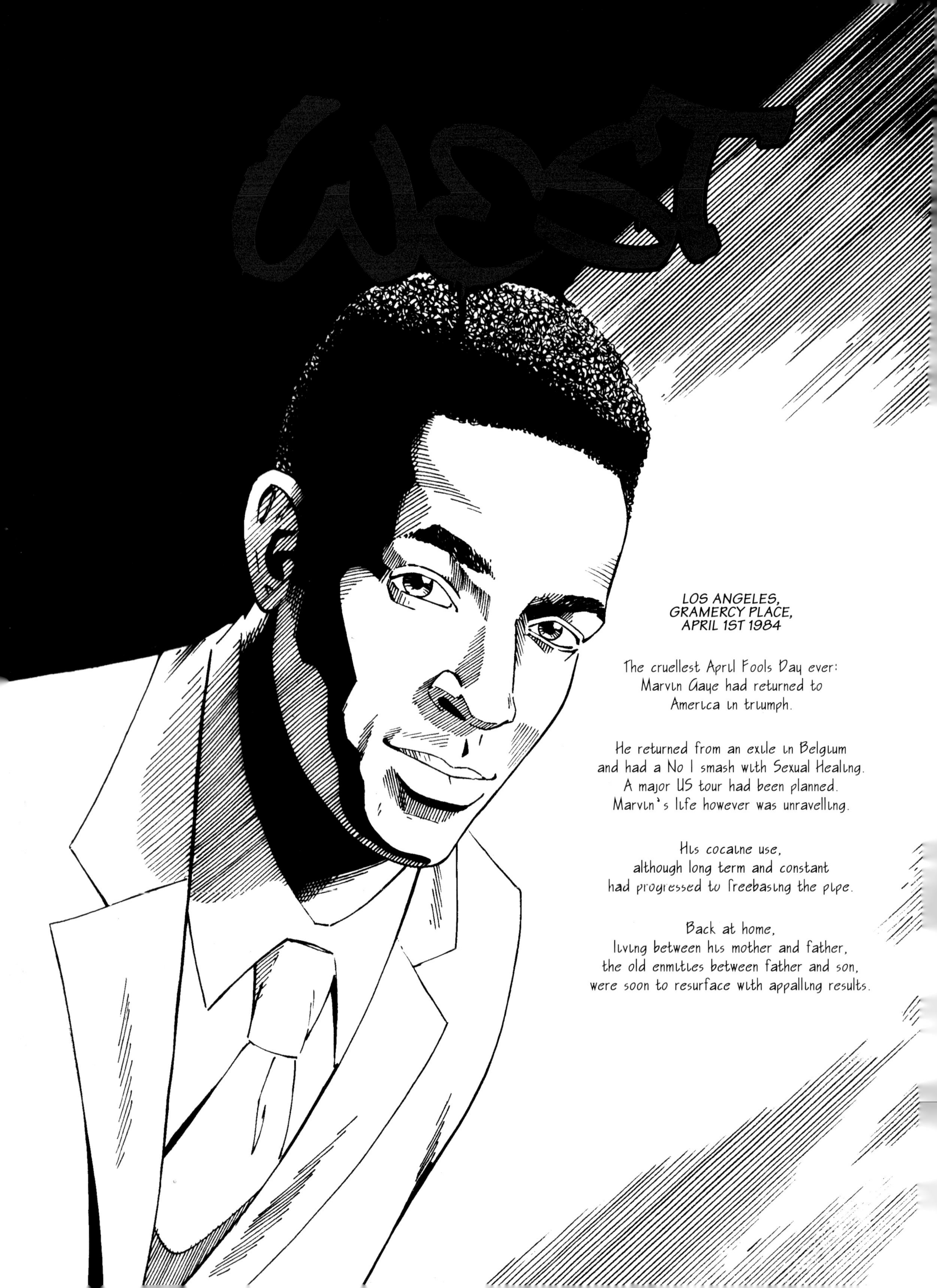
LOS ANGELES, GRAMERCY PLACE, APRIL 1ST 1984
The cruellest April Fools Day ever: Marvin Gaye had returned to America in triumph.
He returned from an exile in Belgium and had a No 1 smash with Sexual Healing. A major US tour had been planned. Marvin's life however was unravelling.
His cocaine use, although long term and constant had progressed to freebasing the pipe.
Back at home, living between his mother and father, the old enmities between father and son, were soon to resurface with appalling results.

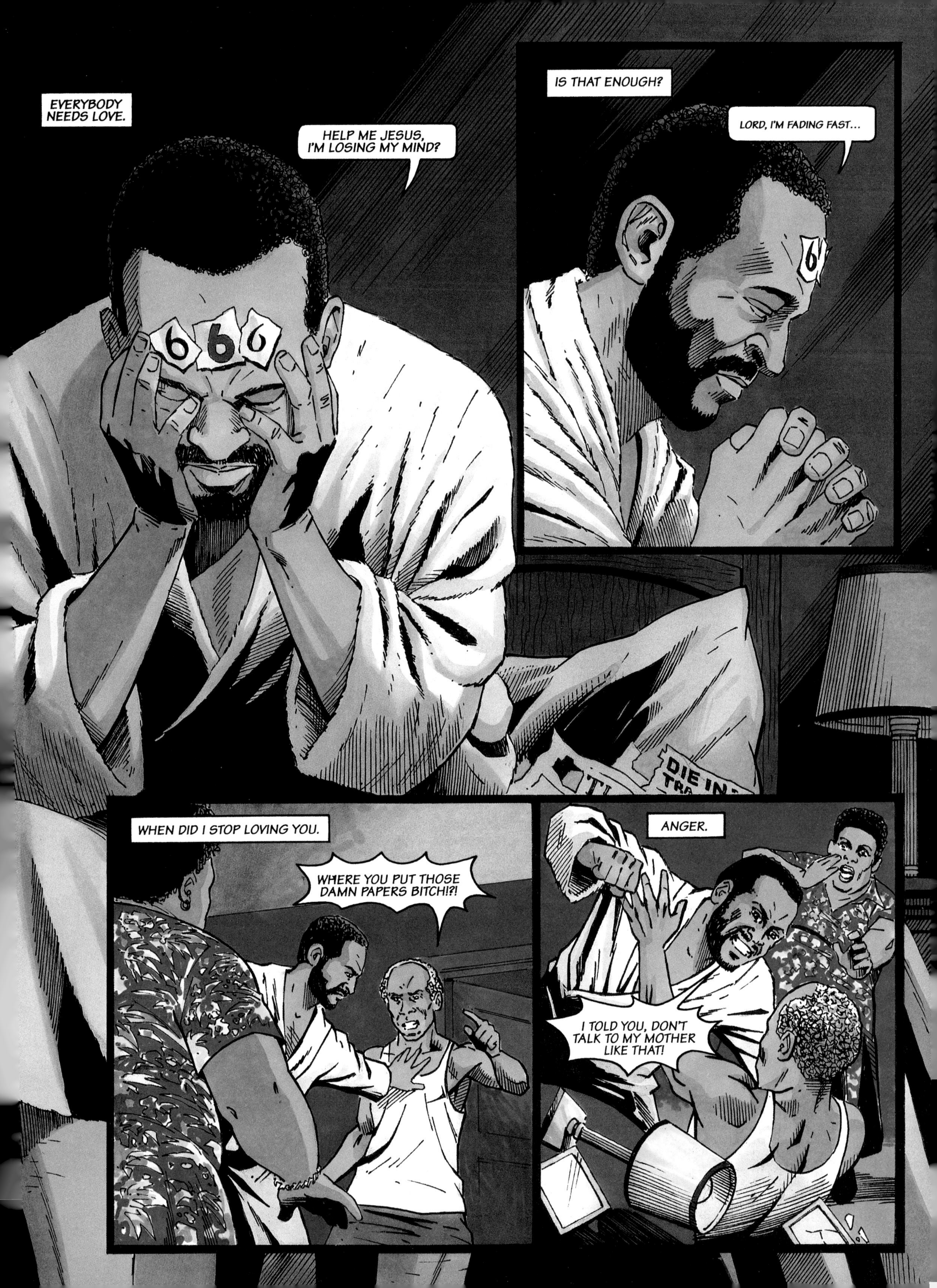
EVERYBODY NEEDS LOVE.
HELP ME JESUS, I'M LOSING MY MIND?
IS THAT ENOUGH?
LORD, I'M FADING FAST...
WHEN DID I STOP LOVING YOU.
WHERE YOU PUT THOSE DAMN PAPERS BITCH!?!
ANGER.
I TOLD YOU, DON'T TALK TO MY MOTHER LIKE THAT!

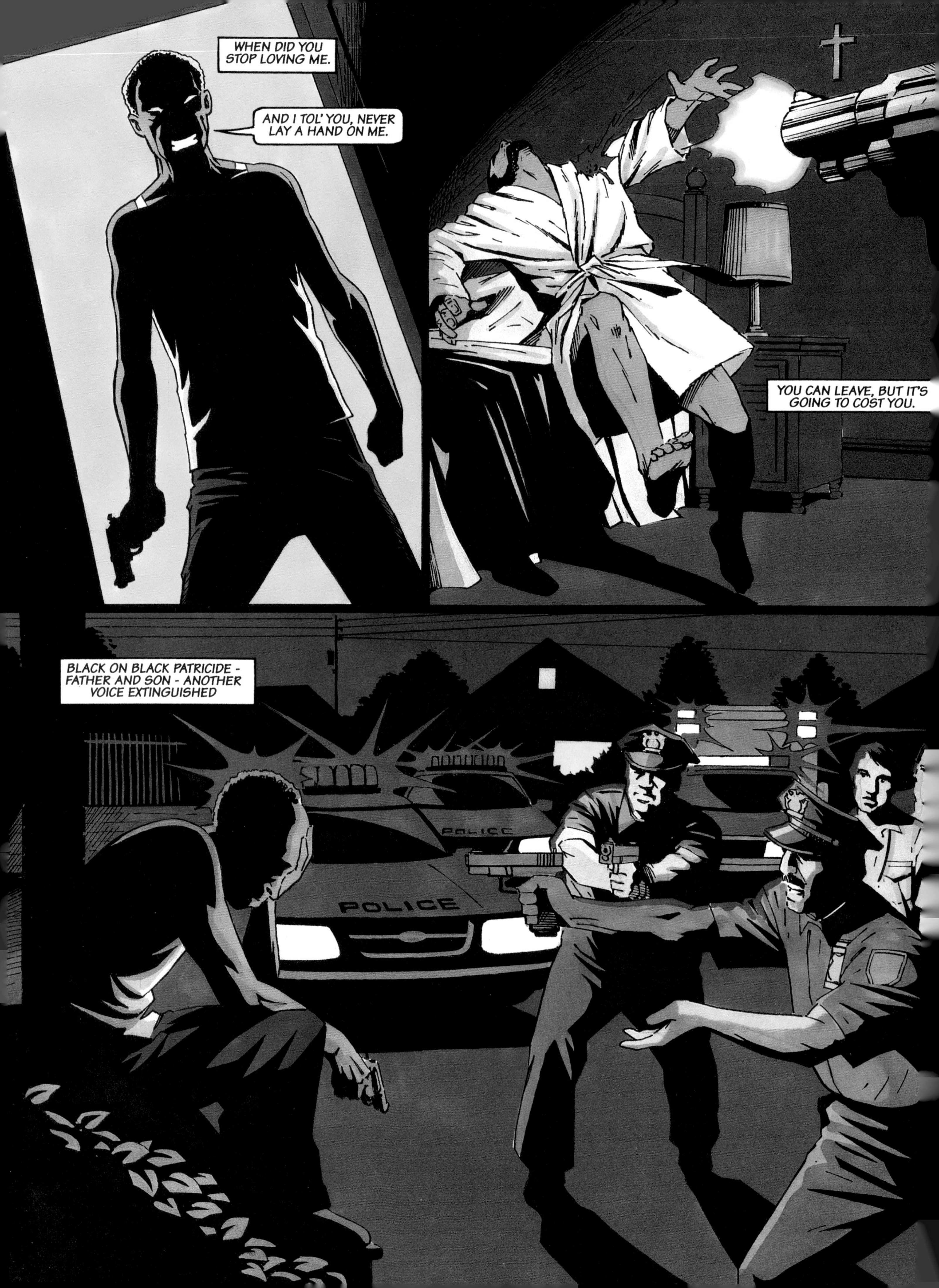
WHEN DID YOU STOP LOVING ME.
AND I TOL' YOU, NEVER LAY A HAND ON ME.
YOU CAN LEAVE, BUT IT'S GOING TO COST YOU.
BLACK ON BLACK PATRICIDE - FATHER AND SON - ANOTHER VOICE EXTINGUISHED
POLICE
POLICE

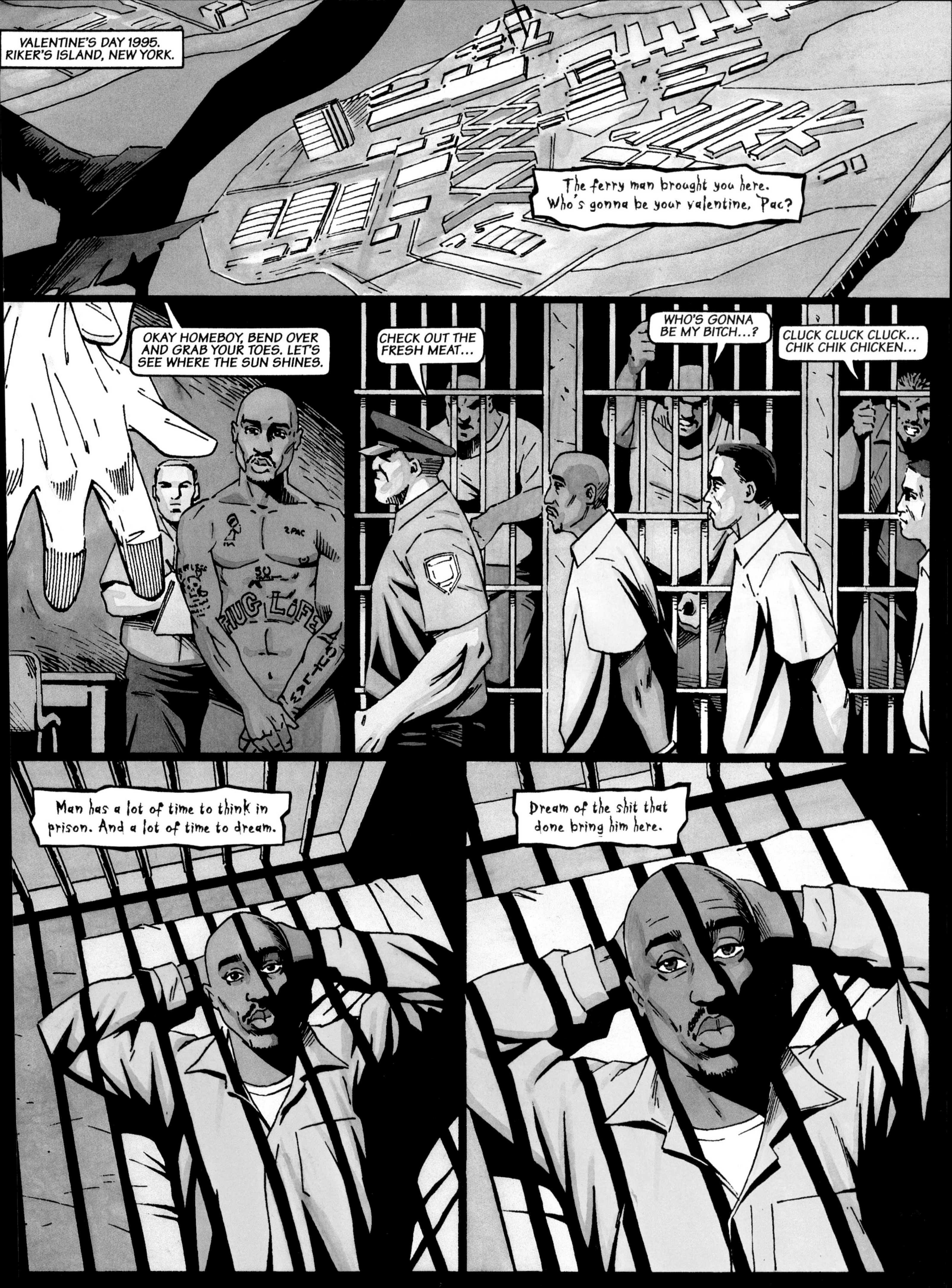
VALENTINE'S DAY 1995. RIKER'S ISLAND, NEW YORK.
The ferry man brought you here. Who's gonna be your valentine, Pac?
OKAY HOMEBOY, BEND OVER AND GRAB YOUR TOES. LET'S SEE WHERE THE SUN SHINES.
CHECK OUT THE FRESH MEAT...
WHO'S GONNA BE MY BITCH...?
CLUCK CLUCK CLUCK... CHIK CHIK CHICKEN...
Man has a lot of time to think in prison. And a lot of time to dream.
Dream of the shit that done bring him here.

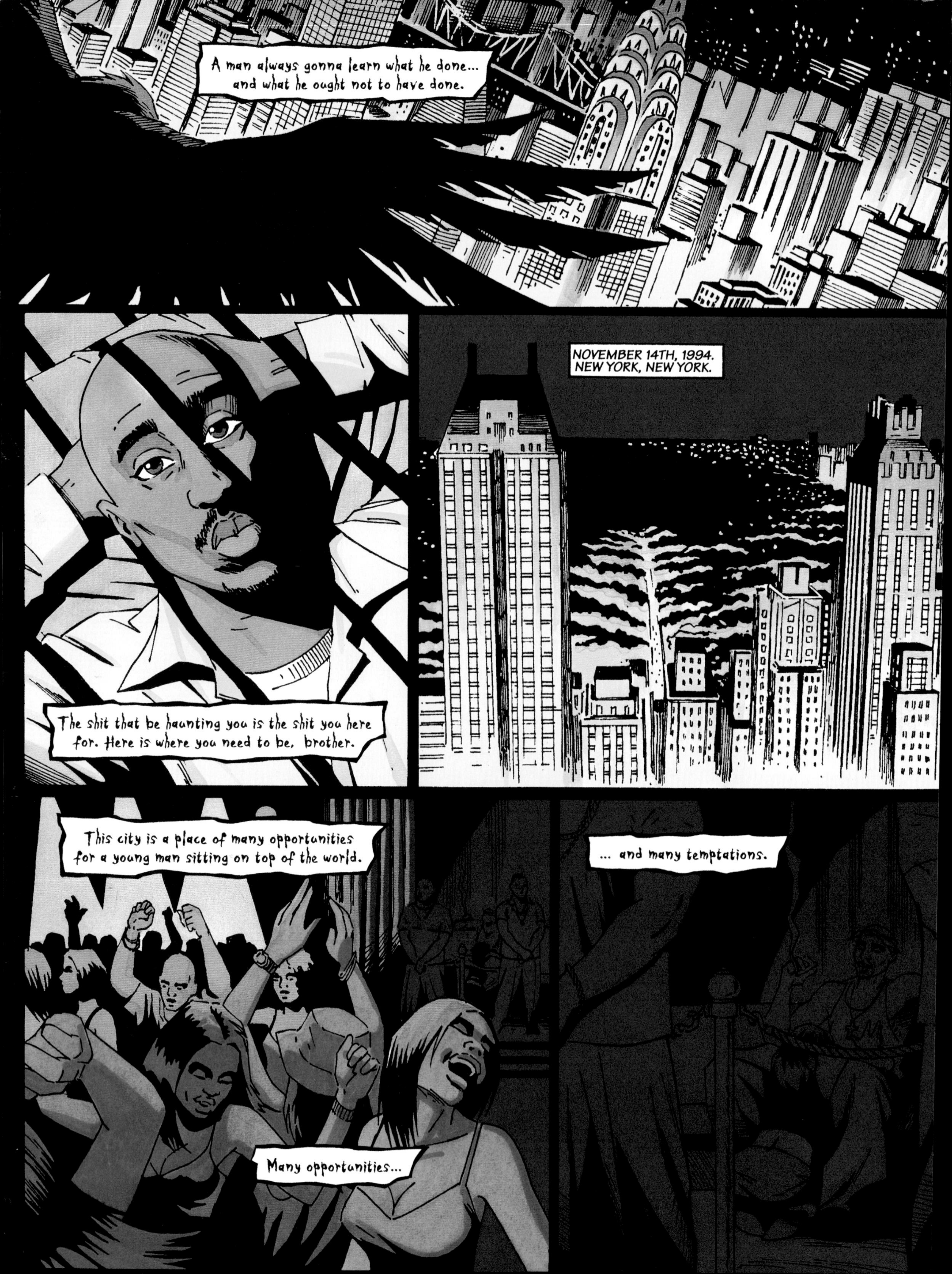
A man always gonna learn what he done... and what he ought not to have done.
The shit that be haunting you is the shit you here for. Here is where you need to be, brother.
NOVEMBER 14TH, 1994. NEW YORK, NEW YORK.
This city is a place of many opportunities for a young man sitting on top of the world.
Many opportunities...
... and many temptations.

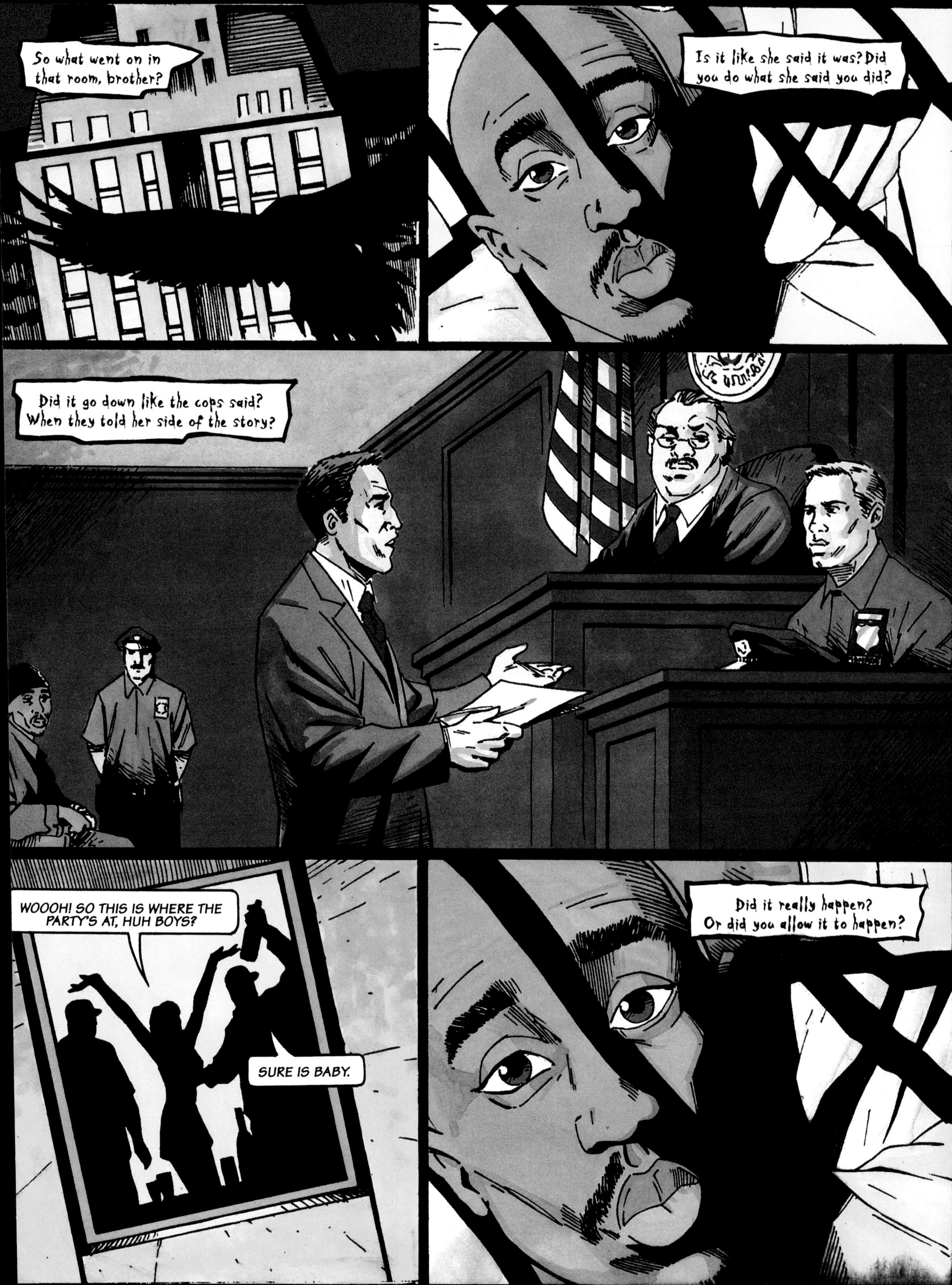
So what went on in that room, brother?
Is it like she said it was? Did you do what she said you did?
Did it go down like the cops said? When they told her side of the story?
WOOOH! SO THIS IS WHERE THE PARTY'S AT, HUH BOYS?
SURE IS BABY.
Did it really happen? Or did you allow it to happen?

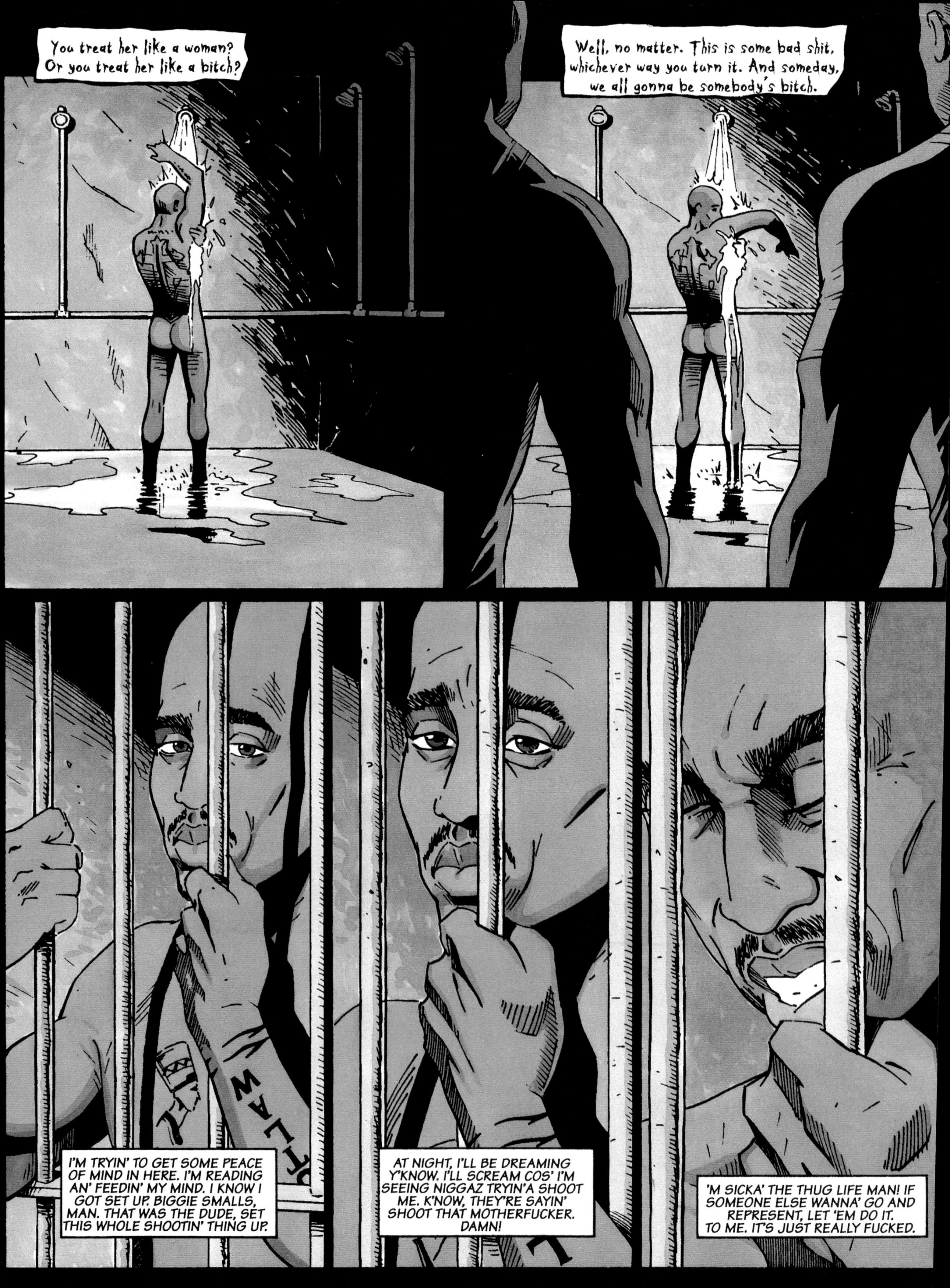
You treat her like a woman? Or you treat her like a bitch?
Well, no matter. This is some bad shit, whichever way you turn it. And someday, we all gonna be somebody's bitch.
I'M TRYIN' TO GET SOME PEACE OF MIND IN HERE. I'M READING AN' FEEDIN' MY MIND. I KNOW I GOT SET UP. BIGGIE SMALLS, MAN. THAT WAS THE DUDE, SET THIS WHOLE SHOOTIN' THING UP.
AT NIGHT, I'LL BE DREAMING Y'KNOW. I'LL SCREAM COS' I'M SEEING NIGGAZ TRYIN'A SHOOT ME. K'NOW, THEY'RE SAYIN' SHOOT THAT MOTHERFUCKER. DAMN!
'M SICKA' THE THUG LIFE MAN! IF SOMEONE ELSE WANNA' GO AND REPRESENT, LET 'EM DO IT. TO ME. IT'S JUST REALLY FUCKED.

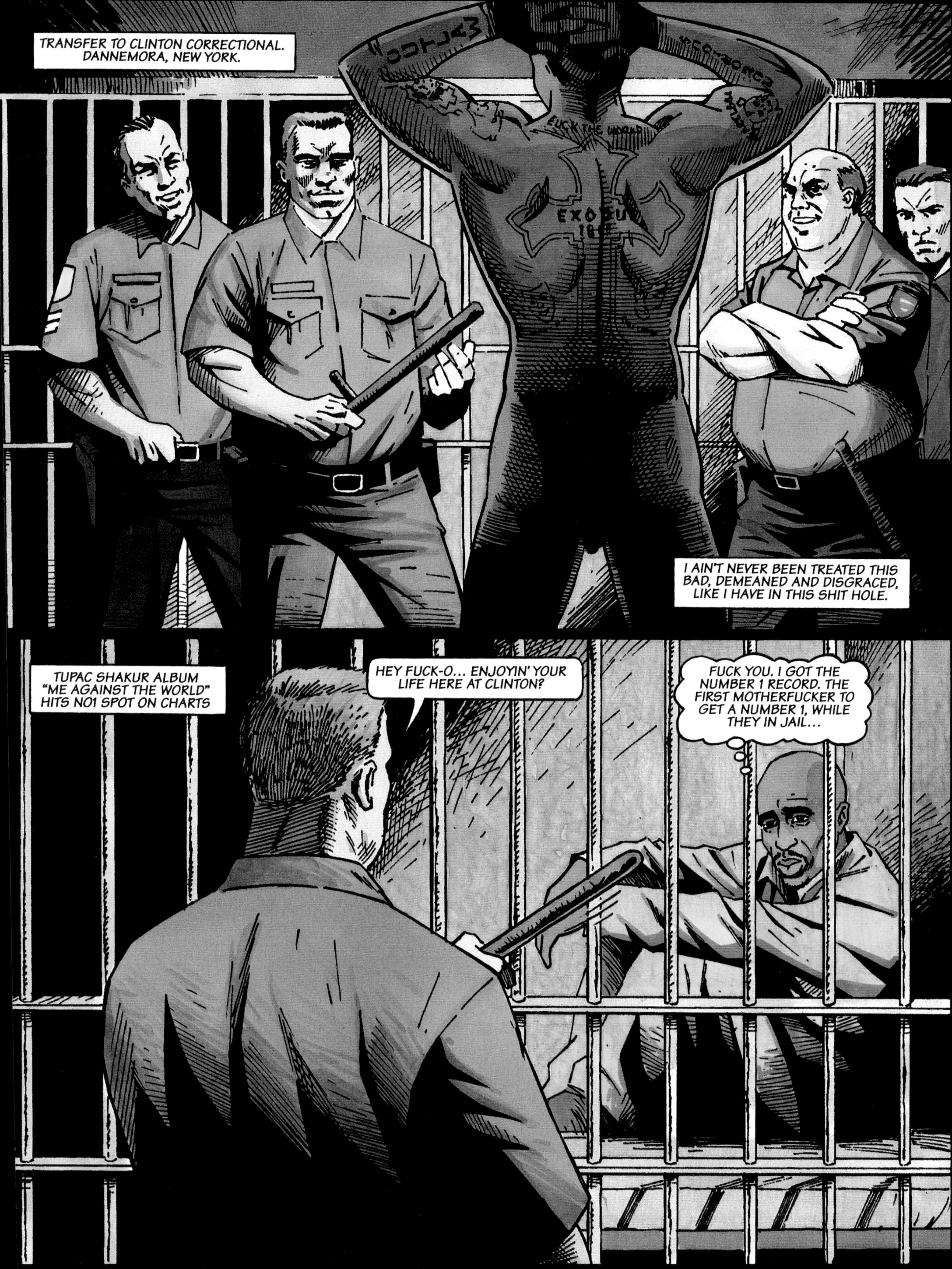
TRANSFER TO CLINTON CORRECTIONAL. DANNEMORA, NEW YORK.
I AIN'T NEVER BEEN TREATED THIS BAD, DEMEANED AND DISGRACED, LIKE I HAVE IN THIS SHIT HOLE.
TUPAC SHAKUR ALBUM "ME AGAINST THE WORLD" HITS NO1 SPOT ON CHARTS
HEY FUCK-O… ENJOYIN' YOUR LIFE HERE AT CLINTON?
FUCK YOU. I GOT THE NUMBER 1 RECORD. THE FIRST MOTHERFUCKER TO GET A NUMBER 1, WHILE THEY IN JAIL…

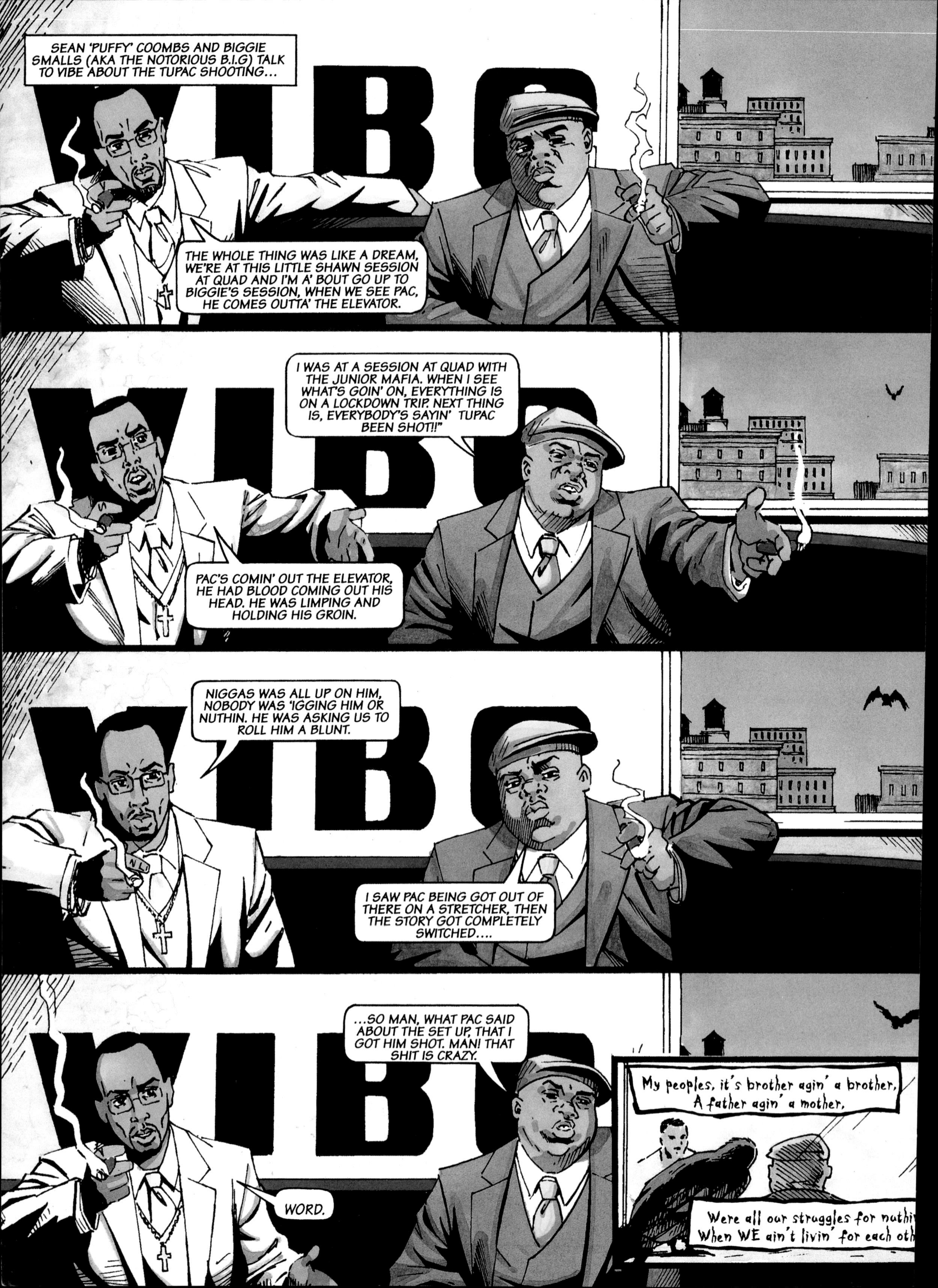
SEAN 'PUFFY' COOMBS AND BIGGIE SMALLS (AKA THE NOTORIOUS B.I.G) TALK TO VIBE ABOUT THE TUPAC SHOOTING...
THE WHOLE THING WAS LIKE A DREAM, WE'RE AT THIS LITTLE SHAWN SESSION AT QUAD AND I'M A' BOUT GO UP TO BIGGIE'S SESSION, WHEN WE SEE PAC, HE COMES OUTTA' THE ELEVATOR.
I WAS AT A SESSION AT QUAD WITH THE JUNIOR MAFIA. WHEN I SEE WHAT'S GOIN' ON, EVERYTHING IS ON A LOCKDOWN TRIP. NEXT THING IS, EVERYBODY'S SAYIN' TUPAC BEEN SHOT!!"
PAC'S COMIN' OUT THE ELEVATOR, HE HAD BLOOD COMING OUT HIS HEAD. HE WAS LIMPING AND HOLDING HIS GROIN.
NIGGAS WAS ALL UP ON HIM, NOBODY WAS 'IGGING HIM OR NUTHIN. HE WAS ASKING US TO ROLL HIM A BLUNT.
I SAW PAC BEING GOT OUT OF THERE ON A STRETCHER, THEN THE STORY GOT COMPLETELY SWITCHED....
...SO MAN, WHAT PAC SAID ABOUT THE SET UP, THAT I GOT HIM SHOT. MAN! THAT SHIT IS CRAZY.
WORD.
My peoples, it's brother agin' a brother, A father agin' a mother.
Were all our struggles for nuthi
When WE ain't livin' for each oth

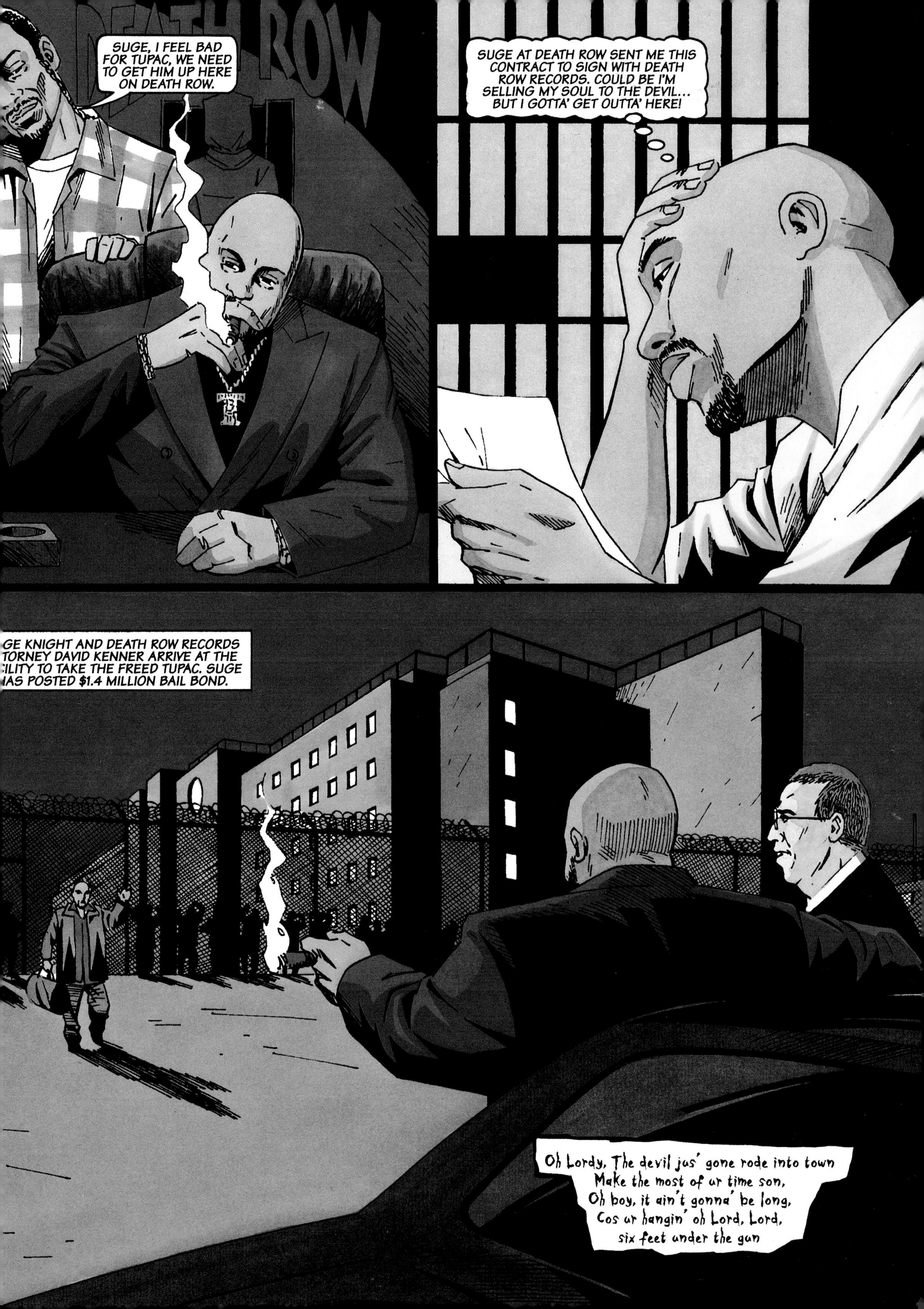
SUGE, I FEEL BAD FOR TUPAC, WE NEED TO GET HIM UP HERE ON DEATH ROW.
SUGE AT DEATH ROW SENT ME THIS CONTRACT TO SIGN WITH DEATH ROW RECORDS. COULD BE I'M SELLING MY SOUL TO THE DEVIL... BUT I GOTTA' GET OUTTA' HERE!
GE KNIGHT AND DEATH ROW RECORDS TORNEY DAVID KENNER ARRIVE AT THE CILITY TO TAKE THE FREED TUPAC. SUGE IAS POSTED $1.4 MILLION BAIL BOND.
Oh Lordy, The devil jus' gone rode into town
Make the most of ur time son,
Oh boy, it ain't gonna' be long,
Cos ur hangin' oh Lord, Lord,
six feet under the gun

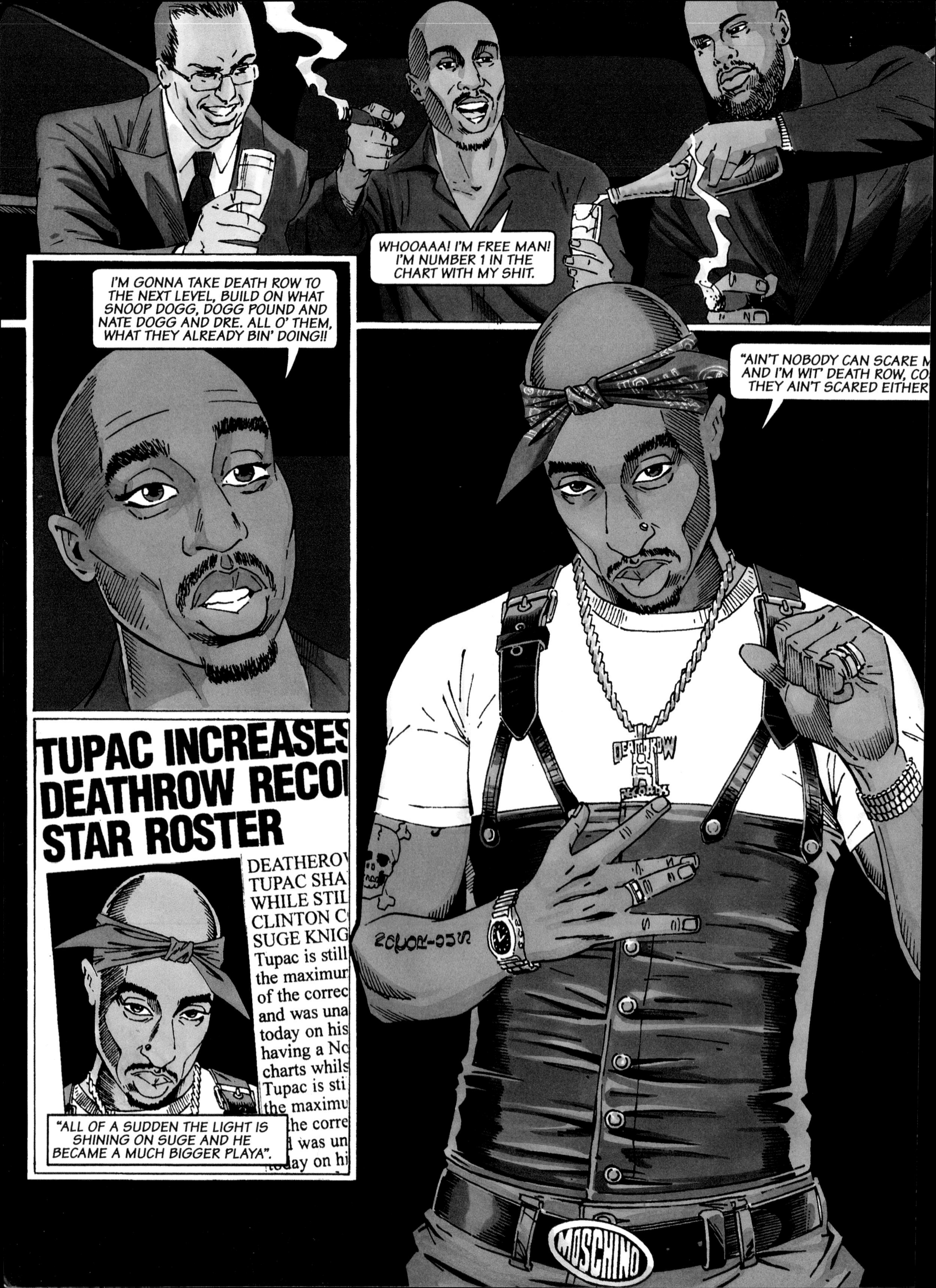
WHOOAAA! I'M FREE MAN! I'M NUMBER 1 IN THE CHART WITH MY SHIT.
I'M GONNA TAKE DEATH ROW TO THE NEXT LEVEL, BUILD ON WHAT SNOOP DOGG, DOGG POUND AND NATE DOGG AND DRE. ALL O' THEM, WHAT THEY ALREADY BIN' DOING!!
"AIN'T NOBODY CAN SCARE M
AND I'M WIT' DEATH ROW, CO
THEY AIN'T SCARED EITHER
TUPAC INCREASES
DEATHROW RECO
STAR ROSTER
DEATHEROV
TUPAC SHA
WHILE STIL
CLINTON C
SUGE KNIG
Tupac is still
the maximur
of the correc
and was una
today on his
having a No
charts whils
Tupac is sti
the maximu
he corre
was un
today on hi
"ALL OF A SUDDEN THE LIGHT IS SHINING ON SUGE AND HE BECAME A MUCH BIGGER PLAYA".
DEATH ROW RECORDS
MOSCHINO

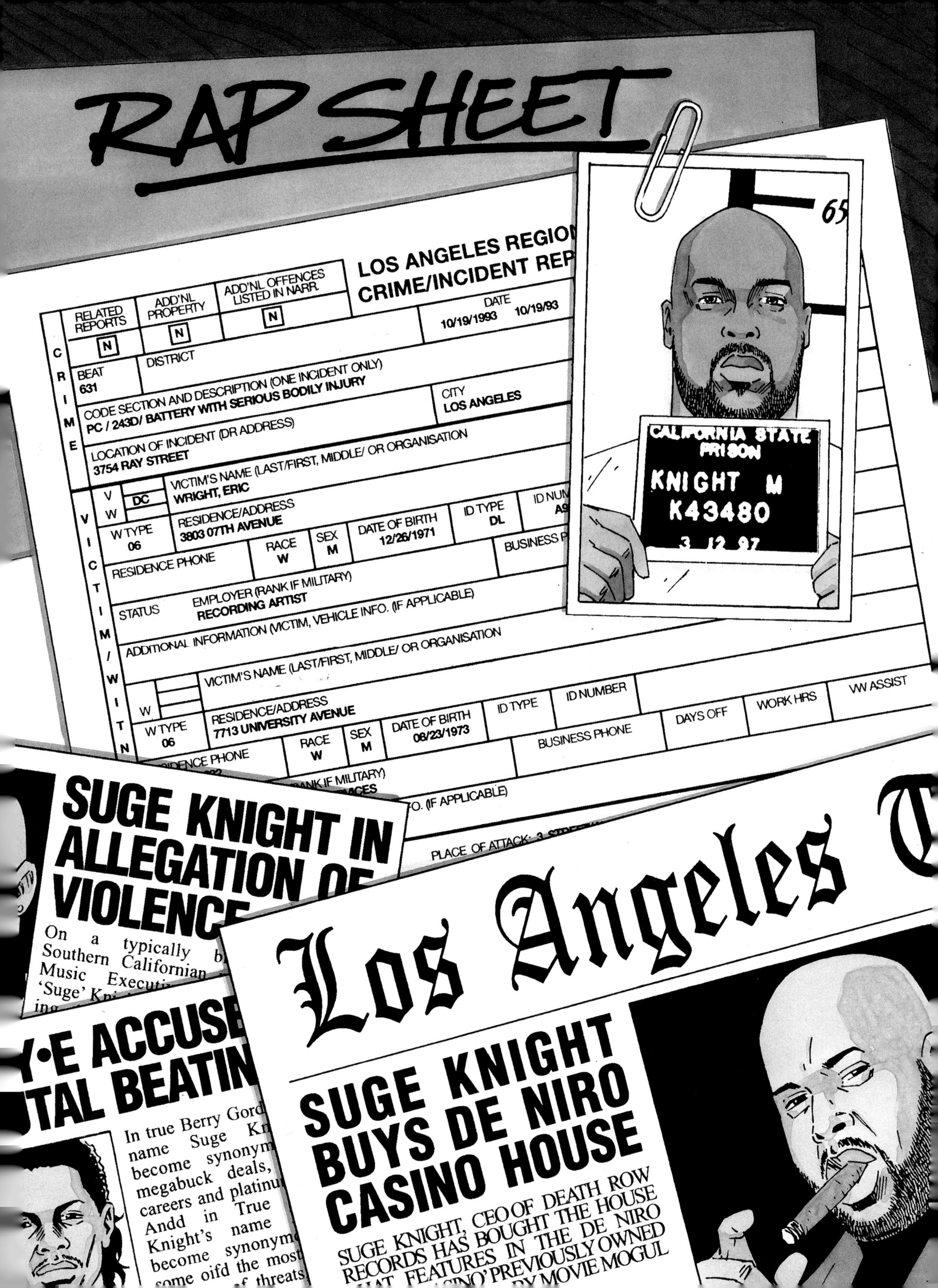
RAP SHEET
LOS ANGELES REGION
CRIME/INCIDENT REP
RELATED REPORTS N
ADD'NL PROPERTY N
ADD'NL OFFENCES LISTED IN NARR. N
DATE 10/19/1993 10/19/93
CRIME
BEAT 631
DISTRICT
CODE SECTION AND DESCRIPTION (ONE INCIDENT ONLY)
PC / 243D/ BATTERY WITH SERIOUS BODILY INJURY
CITY LOS ANGELES
LOCATION OF INCIDENT (DR ADDRESS)
3754 RAY STREET
VICTIM/WITN
V W DC
VICTIM'S NAME (LAST/FIRST, MIDDLE/ OR ORGANISATION
WRIGHT, ERIC
RESIDENCE/ADDRESS 3803 07TH AVENUE
W TYPE 06
DATE OF BIRTH 12/26/1971
ID TYPE DL
RACE W
SEX M
RESIDENCE PHONE
BUSINESS P
STATUS
EMPLOYER (RANK IF MILITARY)
RECORDING ARTIST
ADDITIONAL INFORMATION (VICTIM, VEHICLE INFO. (IF APPLICABLE)
VICTIM'S NAME (LAST/FIRST, MIDDLE/ OR ORGANISATION
W
RESIDENCE/ADDRESS 7713 UNIVERSITY AVENUE
ID TYPE
ID NUMBER
VW ASSIST
W TYPE 06
DATE OF BIRTH 08/23/1973
DAYS OFF
WORK HRS
RACE W
SEX M
BUSINESS PHONE
(IF APPLICABLE)
PLACE OF ATTACK
65
CALIFORNIA STATE PRISON
KNIGHT M
K43480
3 12 97
SUGE KNIGHT IN ALLEGATION OF VIOLENCE
On a typically Southern Californian Music Executive 'Suge' Kni
Los Angeles
ACCUSE
TAL BEATIN
In true Berry Gord name Suge Kn become synonym megabuck deals, careers and platinu Andd in True Knight's name become synonym some oifd the most of threats,
SUGE KNIGHT BUYS DE NIRO CASINO HOUSE
SUGE KNIGHT, CEO OF DEATH ROW RECORDS HAS BOUGHT THE HOUSE THAT FEATURES IN THE DE NIRO 'CASINO' PREVIOUSLY OWNED BY MOVIE MOGUL

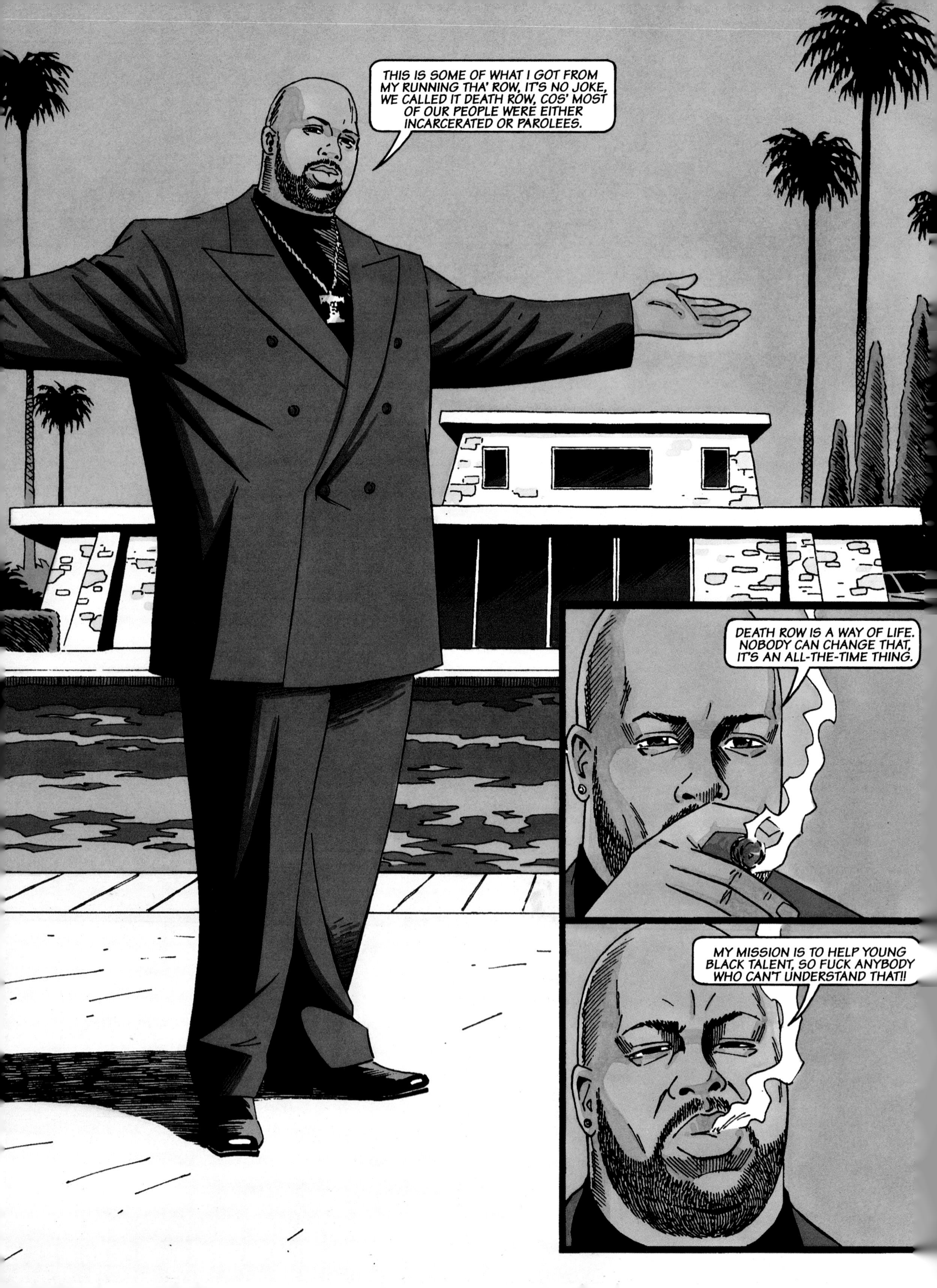
THIS IS SOME OF WHAT I GOT FROM MY RUNNING THA' ROW, IT'S NO JOKE, WE CALLED IT DEATH ROW, COS' MOST OF OUR PEOPLE WERE EITHER INCARCERATED OR PAROLEES.
DEATH ROW IS A WAY OF LIFE. NOBODY CAN CHANGE THAT, IT'S AN ALL-THE-TIME THING.
MY MISSION IS TO HELP YOUNG BLACK TALENT, SO FUCK ANYBODY WHO CAN'T UNDERSTAND THAT!!

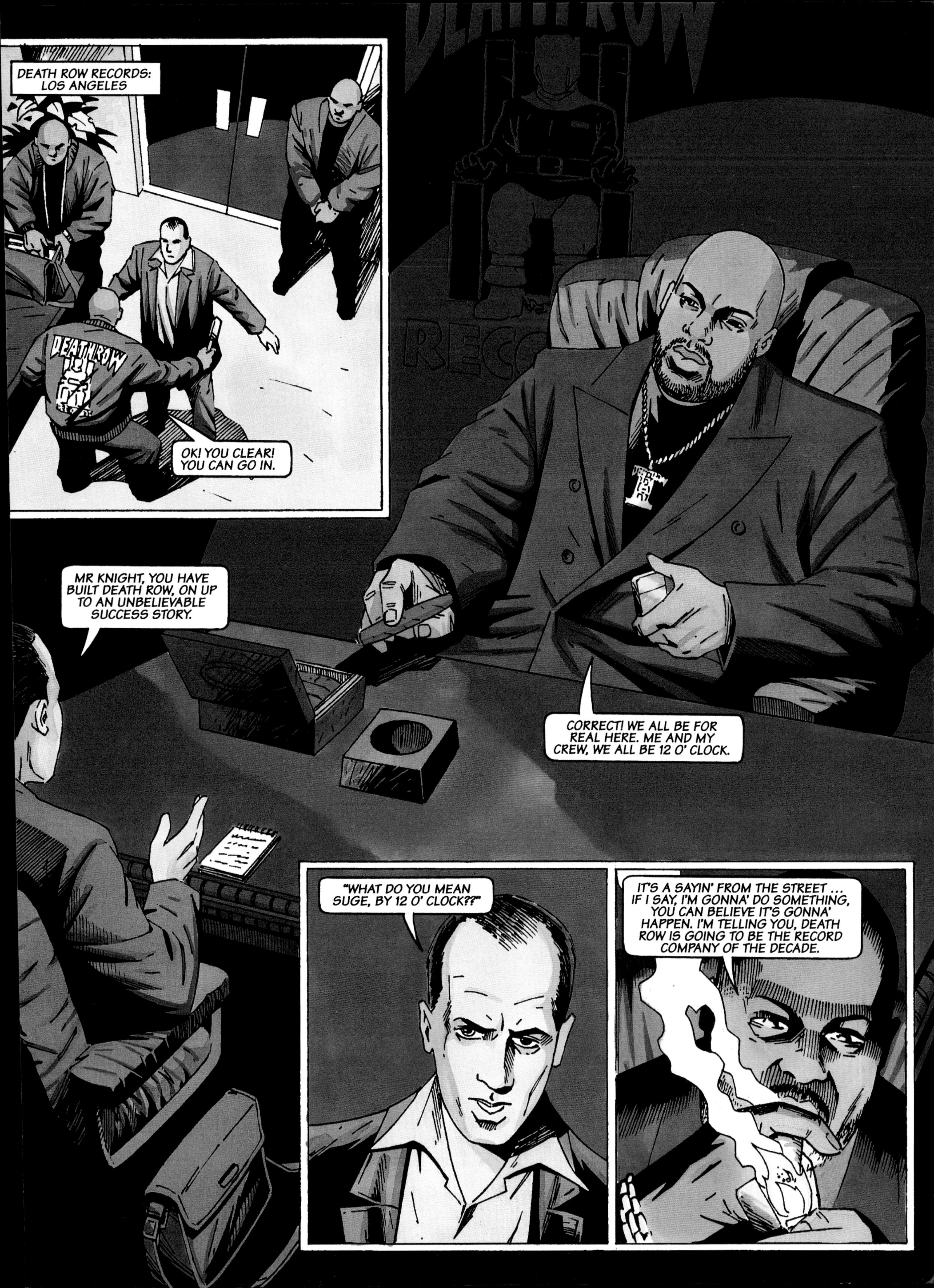
DEATH ROW RECORDS: LOS ANGELES
OK! YOU CLEAR! YOU CAN GO IN.
MR KNIGHT, YOU HAVE BUILT DEATH ROW, ON UP TO AN UNBELIEVABLE SUCCESS STORY.
CORRECT! WE ALL BE FOR REAL HERE. ME AND MY CREW, WE ALL BE 12 O' CLOCK.
"WHAT DO YOU MEAN SUGE, BY 12 O' CLOCK??"
IT'S A SAYIN' FROM THE STREET ... IF I SAY, I'M GONNA' DO SOMETHING, YOU CAN BELIEVE IT'S GONNA' HAPPEN. I'M TELLING YOU, DEATH ROW IS GOING TO BE THE RECORD COMPANY OF THE DECADE.

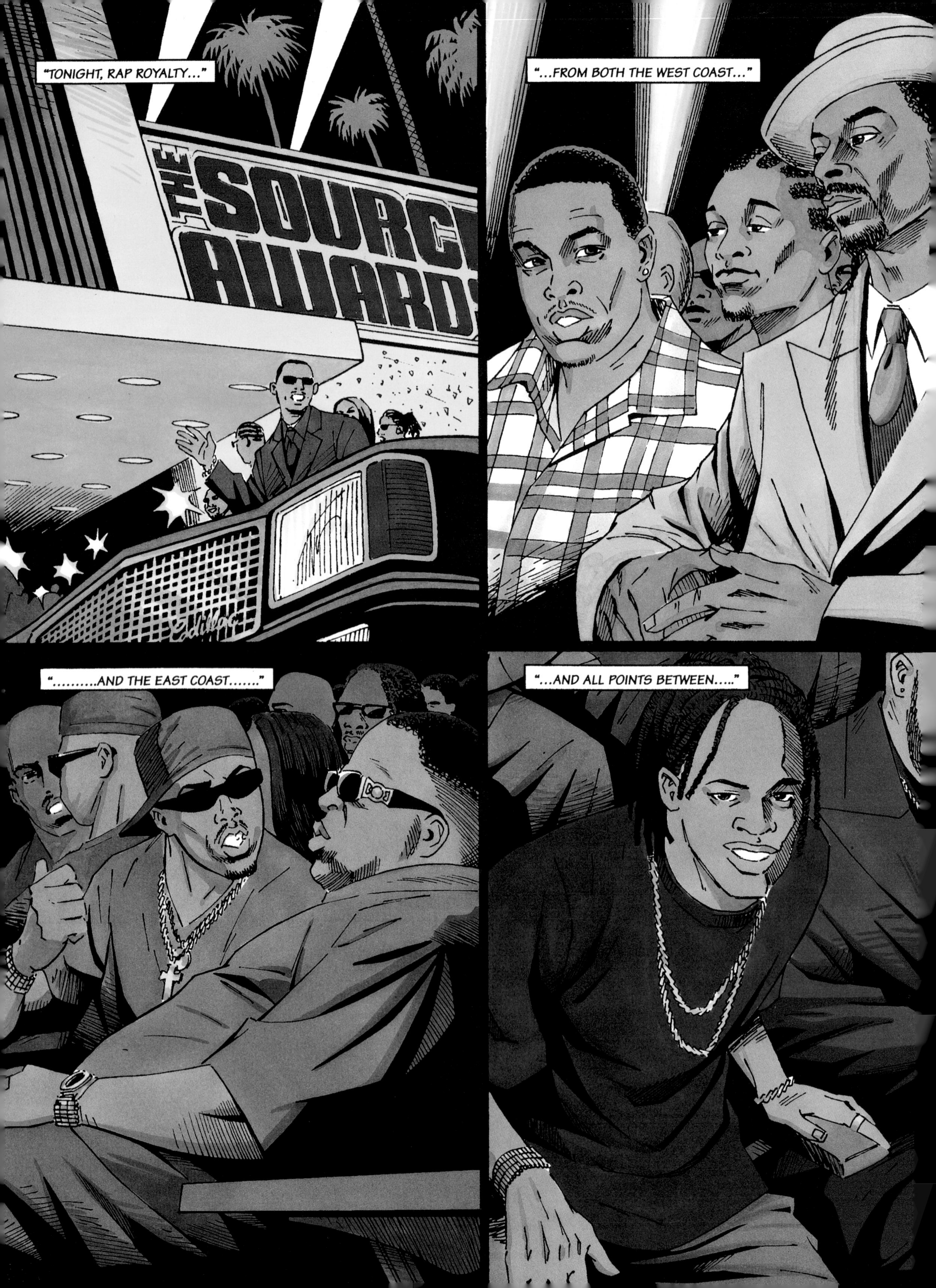
"TONIGHT, RAP ROYALTY..."
THE SOURCE AWARDS
"...FROM BOTH THE WEST COAST..."
"..........AND THE EAST COAST......."
"...AND ALL POINTS BETWEEN....."

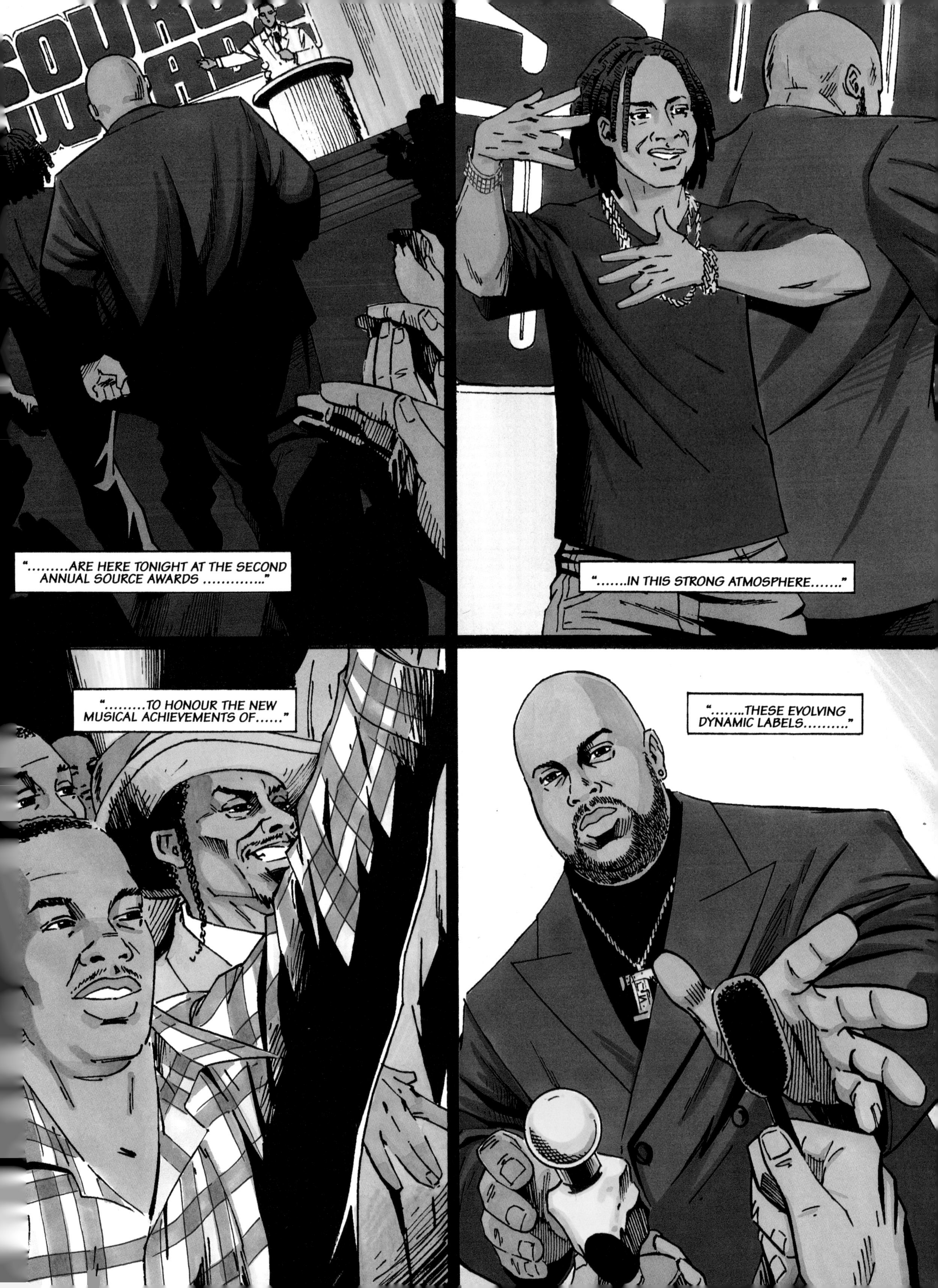
"………ARE HERE TONIGHT AT THE SECOND ANNUAL SOURCE AWARDS ………….."
"……IN THIS STRONG ATMOSPHERE……."
"………TO HONOUR THE NEW MUSICAL ACHIEVEMENTS OF……"
"……..THESE EVOLVING DYNAMIC LABELS………."

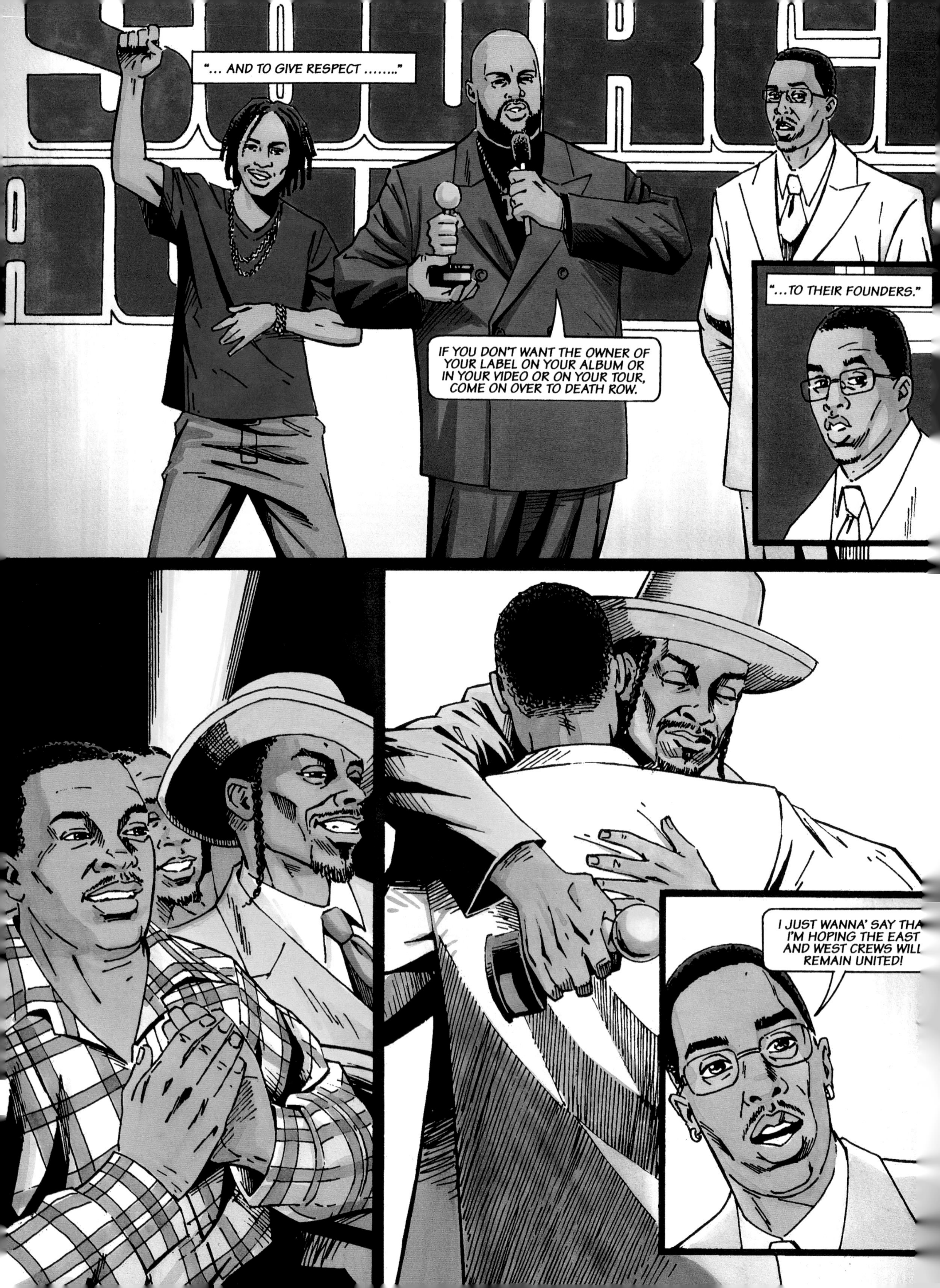
"... AND TO GIVE RESPECT ...."
IF YOU DON'T WANT THE OWNER OF YOUR LABEL ON YOUR ALBUM OR IN YOUR VIDEO OR ON YOUR TOUR, COME ON OVER TO DEATH ROW.
"...TO THEIR FOUNDERS."
I JUST WANNA' SAY THA I'M HOPING THE EAST AND WEST CREWS WILL REMAIN UNITED!

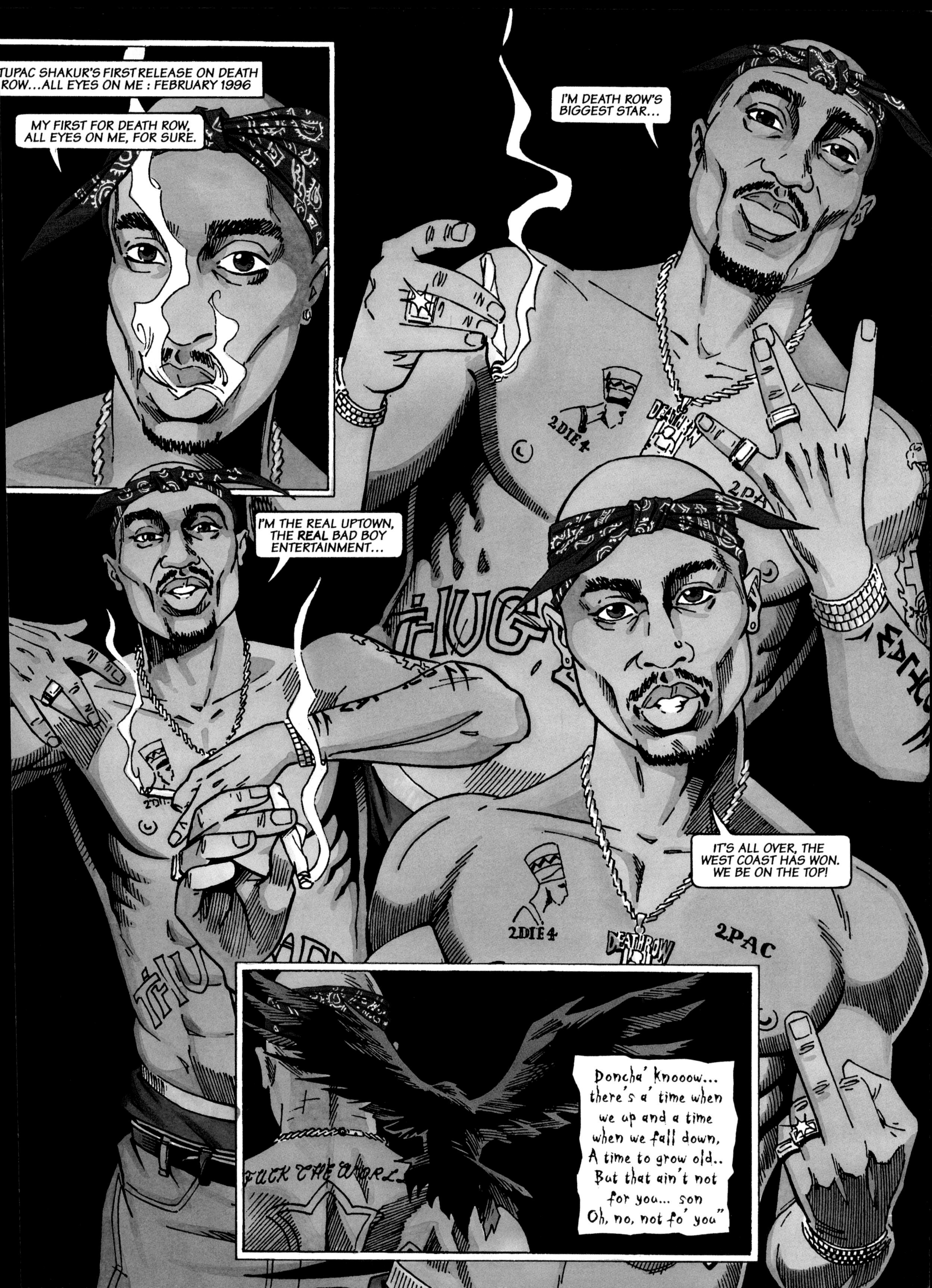
TUPAC SHAKUR'S FIRST RELEASE ON DEATH ROW...ALL EYES ON ME : FEBRUARY 1996
MY FIRST FOR DEATH ROW, ALL EYES ON ME, FOR SURE.
I'M DEATH ROW'S BIGGEST STAR...
I'M THE REAL UPTOWN, THE REAL BAD BOY ENTERTAINMENT...
IT'S ALL OVER, THE WEST COAST HAS WON. WE BE ON THE TOP!
Doncha' knooow... there's a' time when we up and a time when we fall down, A time to grow old.. But that ain't not for you... son Oh, no, not fo' you"

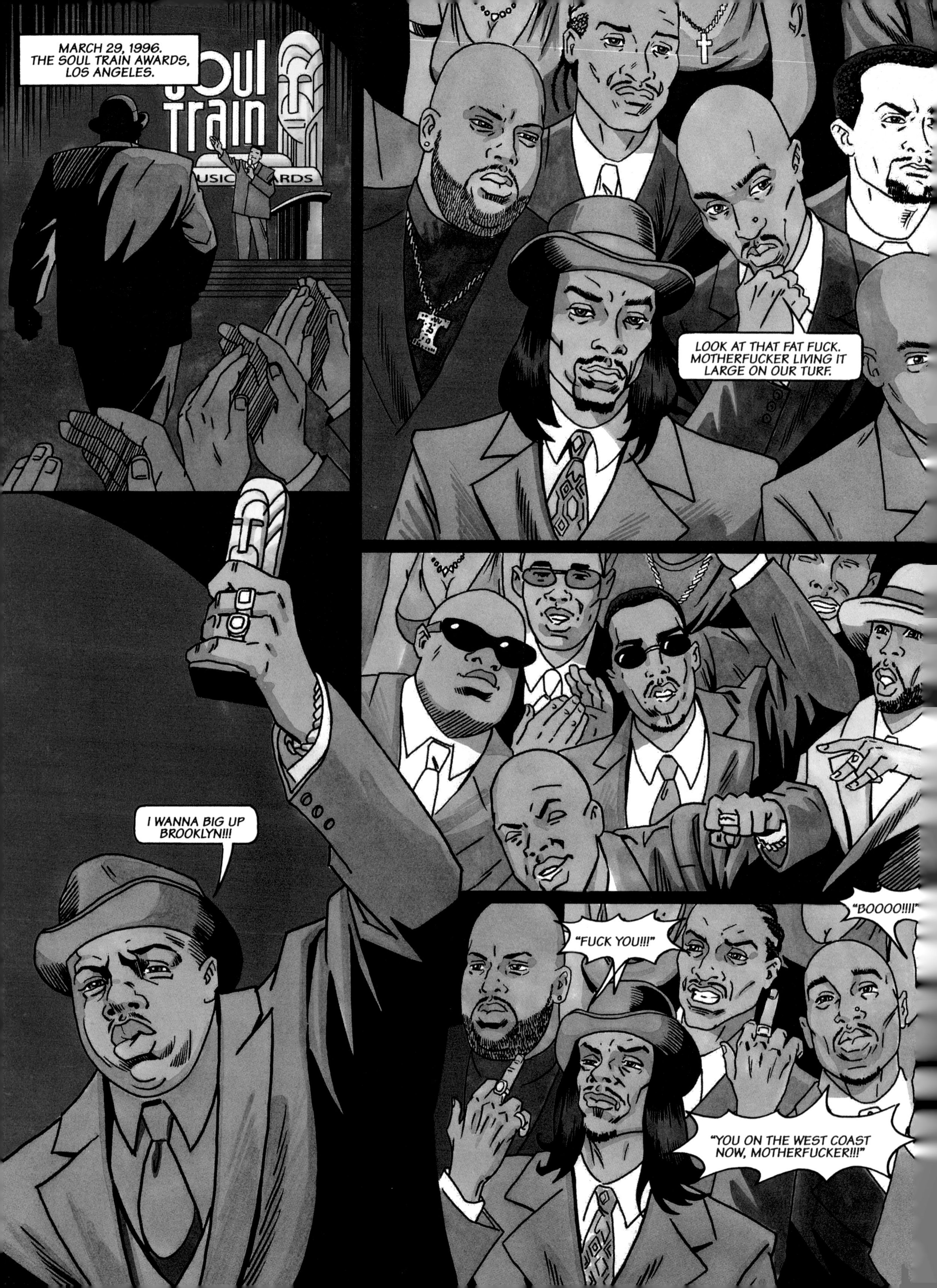

MARCH 29, 1996. THE SOUL TRAIN AWARDS, LOS ANGELES.
SOUL TRAIN
MUSIC AWARDS
LOOK AT THAT FAT FUCK. MOTHERFUCKER LIVING IT LARGE ON OUR TURF.
I WANNA BIG UP BROOKLYN!!!
"FUCK YOU!!!"
"BOOOO!!!!"
"YOU ON THE WEST COAST NOW, MOTHERFUCKER!!!"

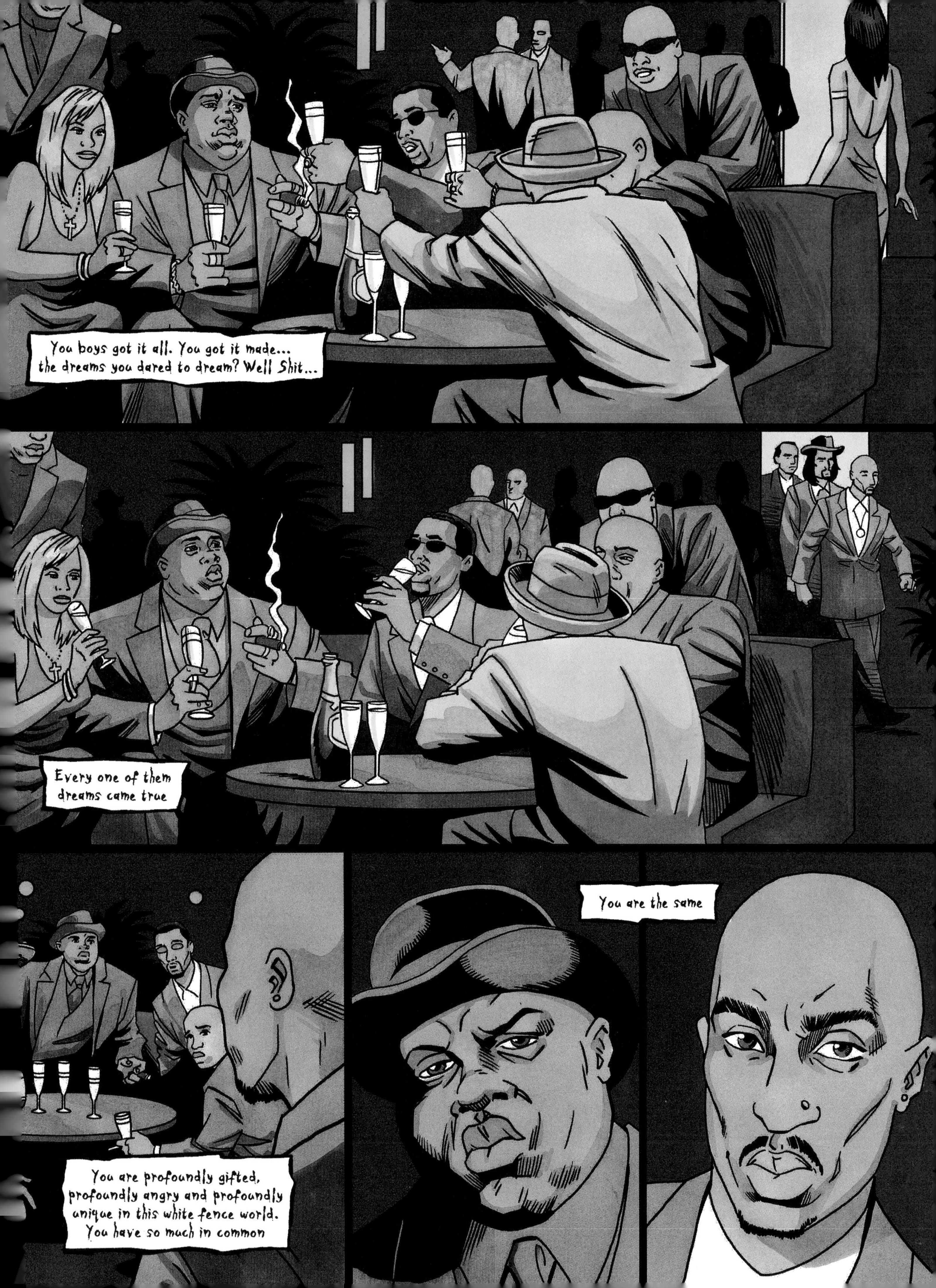
You boys got it all. You got it made... the dreams you dared to dream? Well Shit...
Every one of them dreams came true
You are profoundly gifted, profoundly angry and profoundly unique in this white fence world. You have so much in common
You are the same

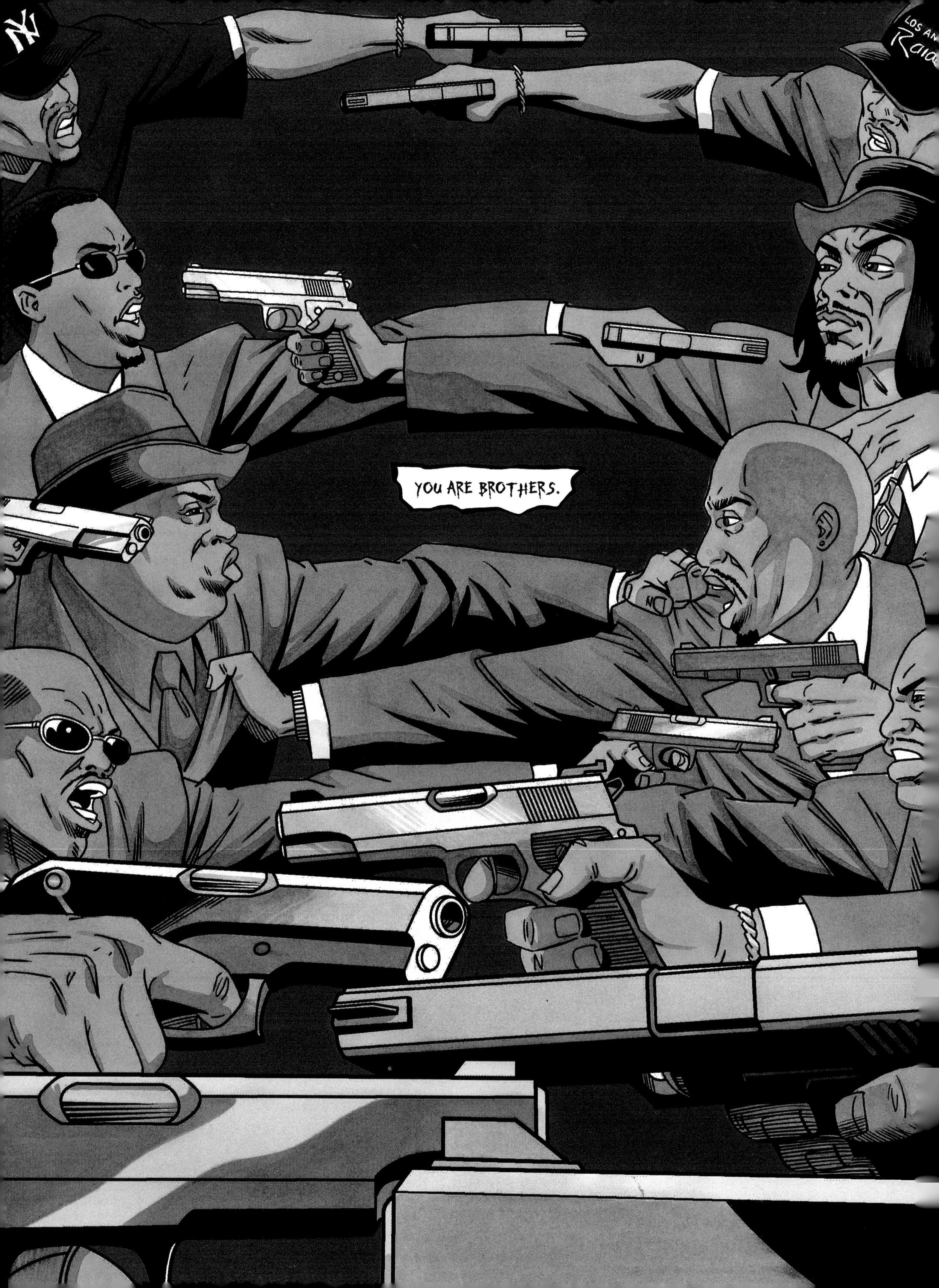
YOU ARE BROTHERS.

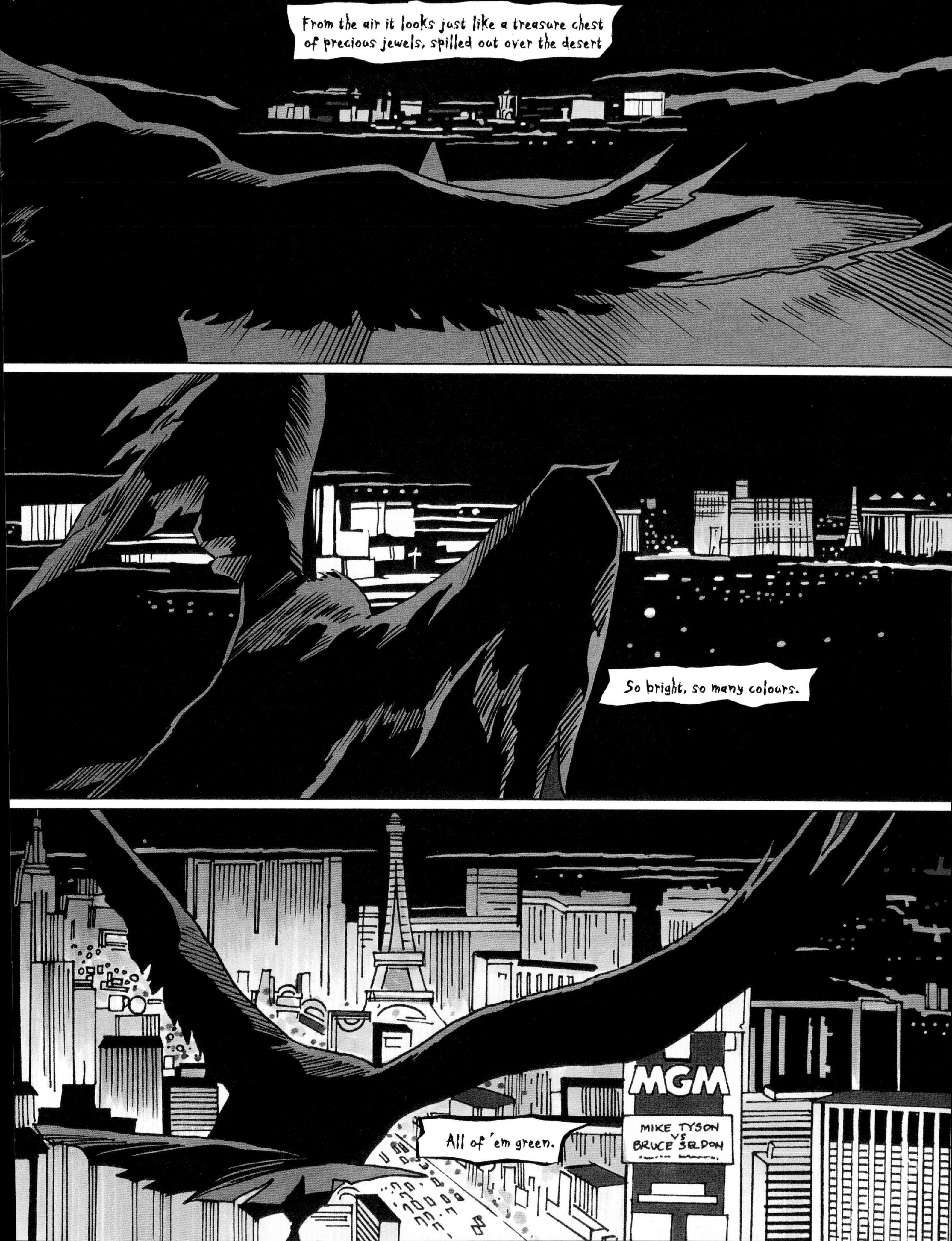
From the air it looks just like a treasure chest of precious jewels, spilled out over the desert
So bright, so many colours.
MGM
MIKE TYSON VS BRUCE SELDON
All of 'em green.

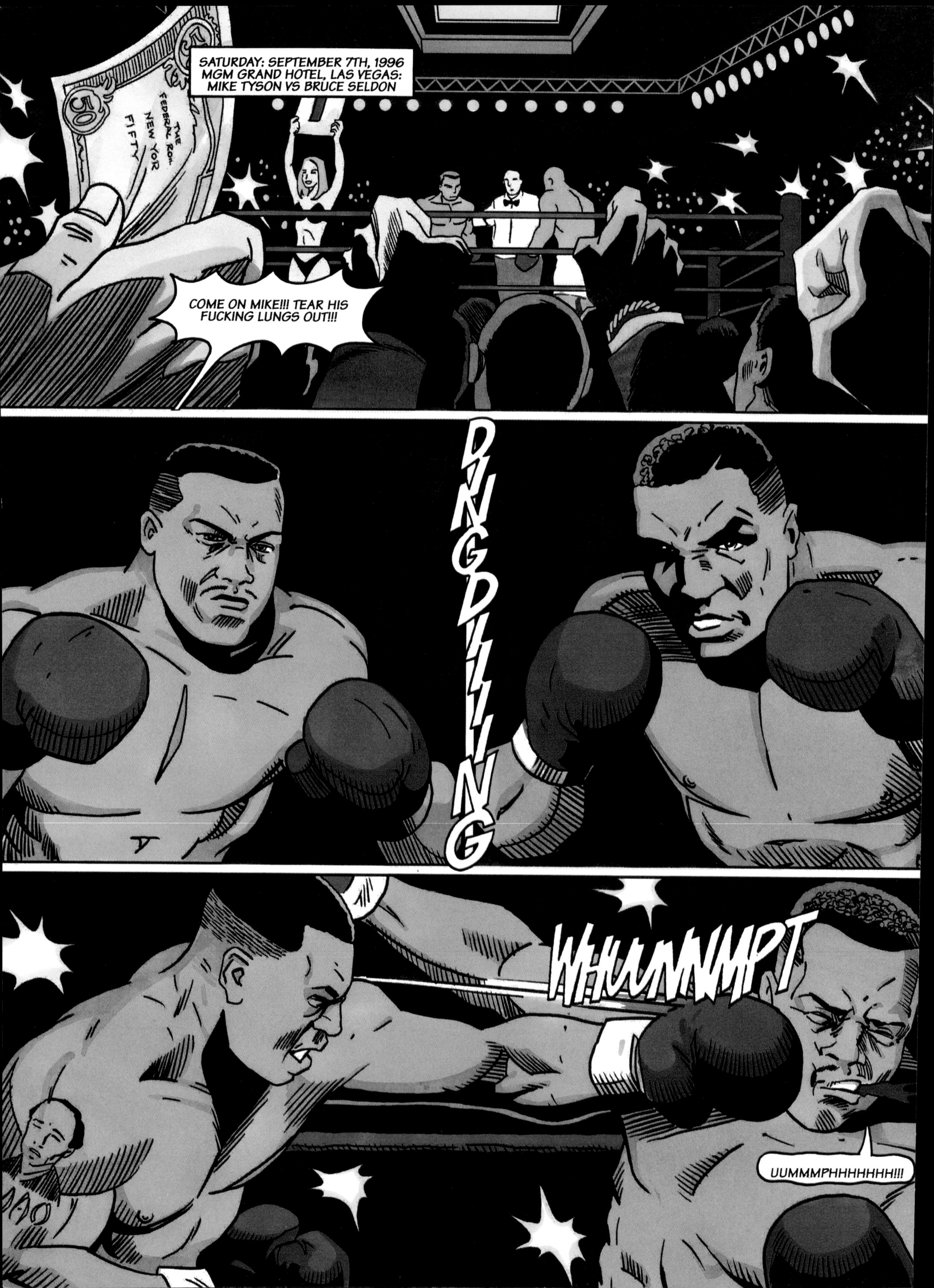

SATURDAY: SEPTEMBER 7TH, 1996
MGM GRAND HOTEL, LAS VEGAS:
MIKE TYSON VS BRUCE SELDON
COME ON MIKE!!! TEAR HIS FUCKING LUNGS OUT!!!
DINGDIIIIING
WHUUNMPT
UUMMMPHHHHHHH!!!

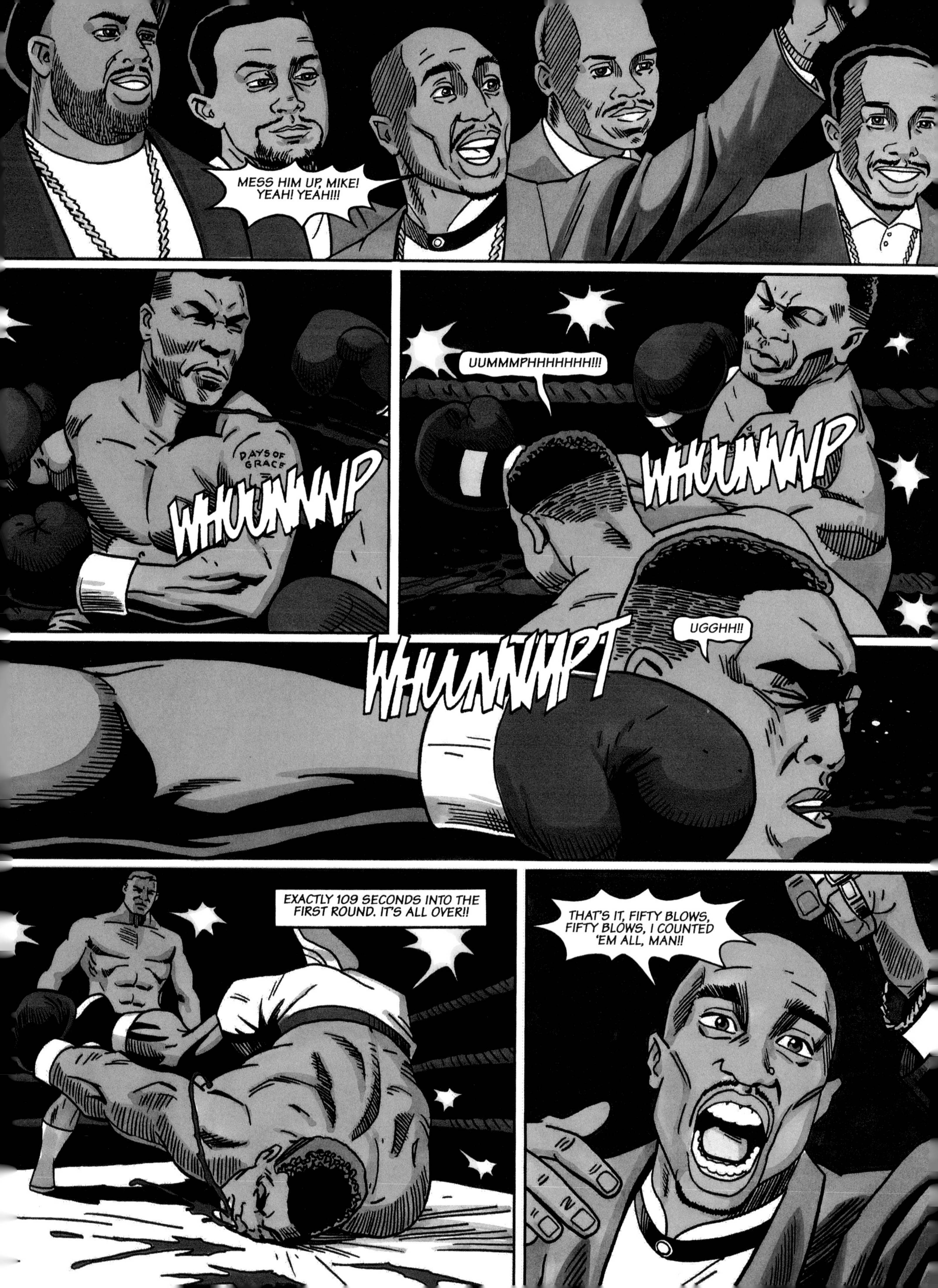

MESS HIM UP, MIKE! YEAH! YEAH!!!
DAYS OF GRACE
WHOUNNWP
UUMMMPHHHHHHH!!!
WHOUNNWP
WHUUNNMPT
UGGHH!!
EXACTLY 109 SECONDS INTO THE FIRST ROUND. IT'S ALL OVER!!
THAT'S IT, FIFTY BLOWS, FIFTY BLOWS, I COUNTED 'EM ALL, MAN!!

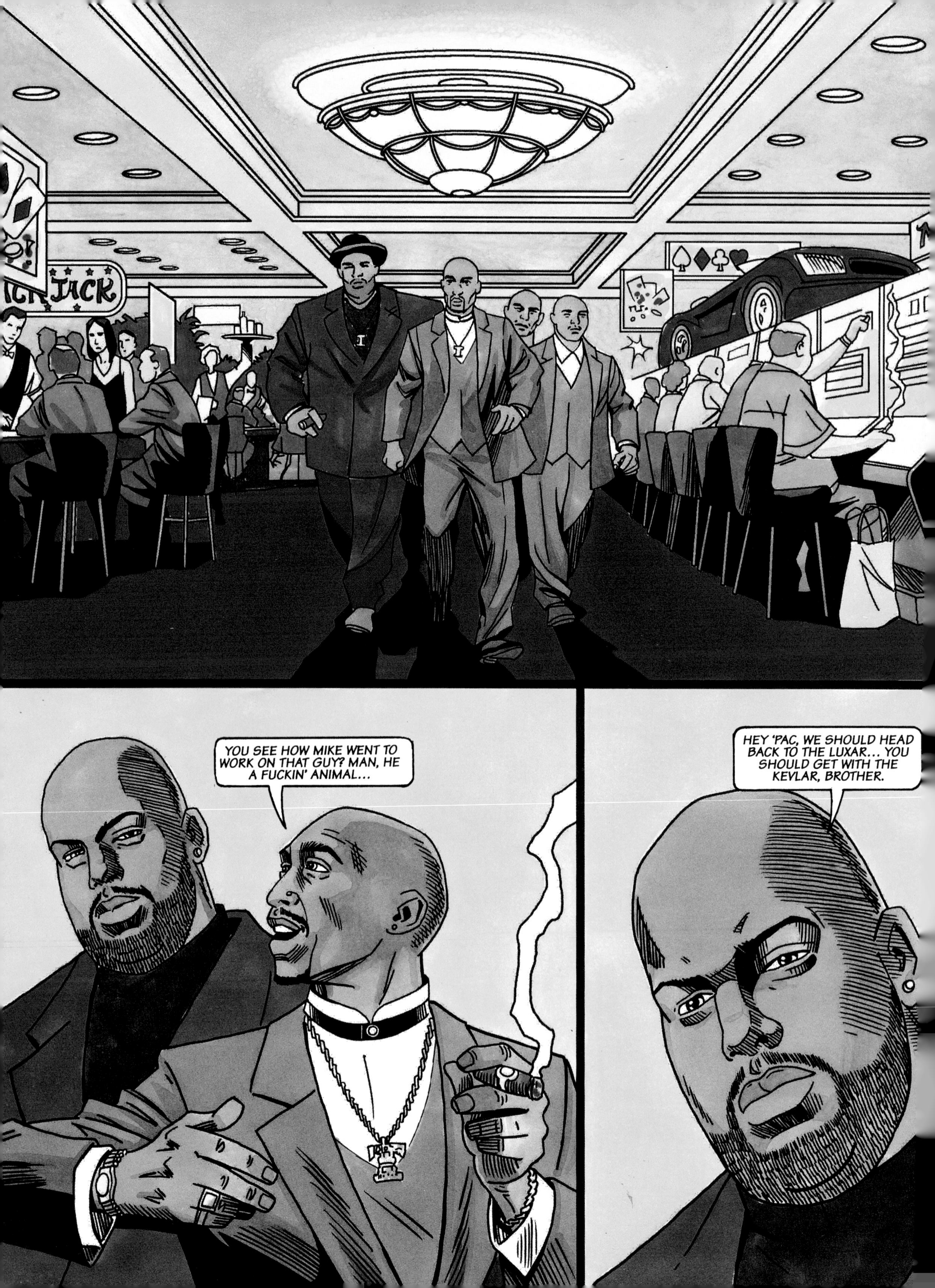
JACK
YOU SEE HOW MIKE WENT TO WORK ON THAT GUY? MAN, HE A FUCKIN' ANIMAL...
HEY 'PAC, WE SHOULD HEAD BACK TO THE LUXAR... YOU SHOULD GET WITH THE KEVLAR, BROTHER.

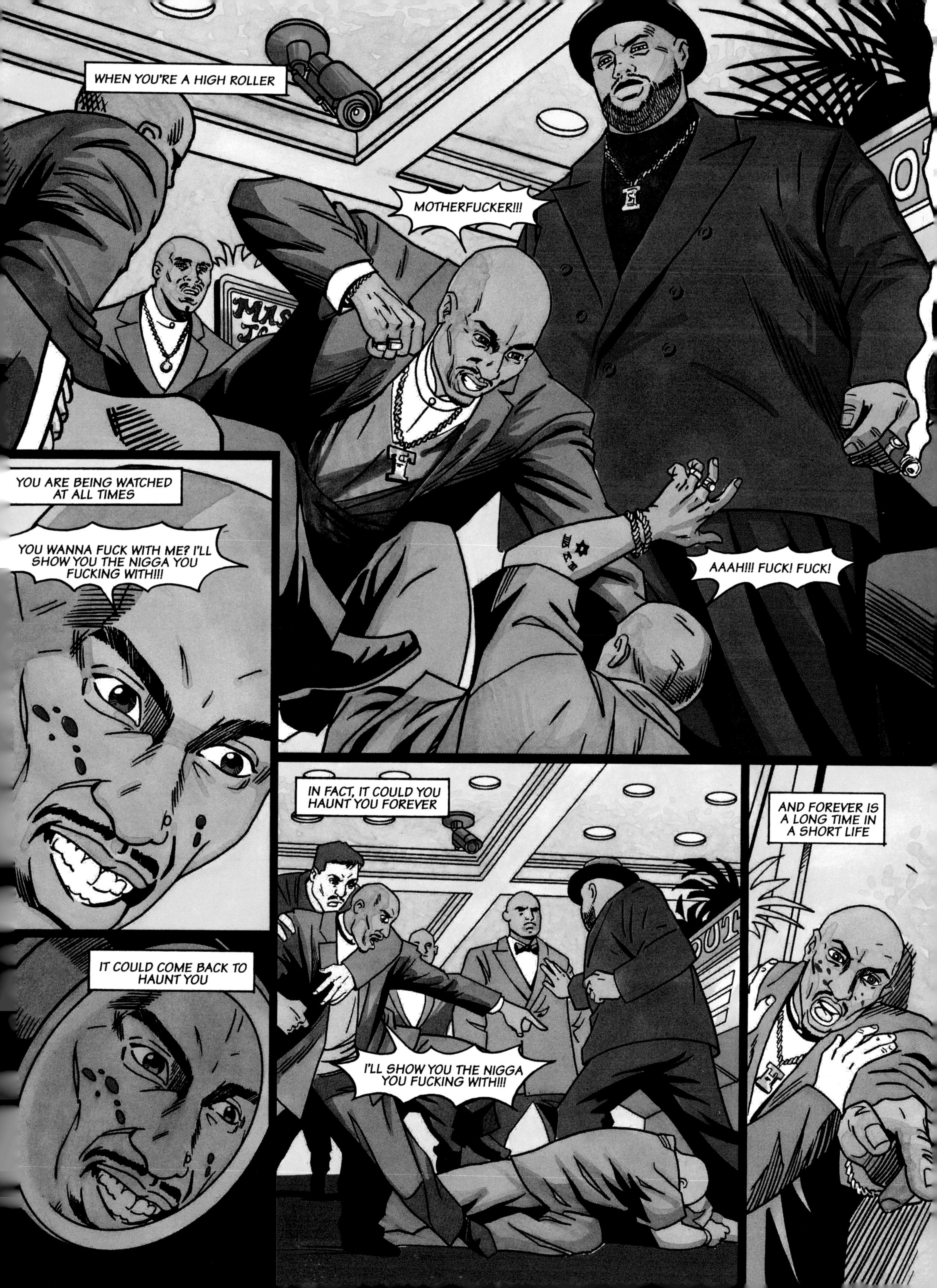
WHEN YOU'RE A HIGH ROLLER
MOTHERFUCKER!!!
AAAH!!! FUCK! FUCK!
YOU ARE BEING WATCHED AT ALL TIMES
YOU WANNA FUCK WITH ME? I'LL SHOW YOU THE NIGGA YOU FUCKING WITH!!!
IT COULD COME BACK TO HAUNT YOU
IN FACT, IT COULD YOU HAUNT YOU FOREVER
I'LL SHOW YOU THE NIGGA YOU FUCKING WITH!!!
AND FOREVER IS A LONG TIME IN A SHORT LIFE

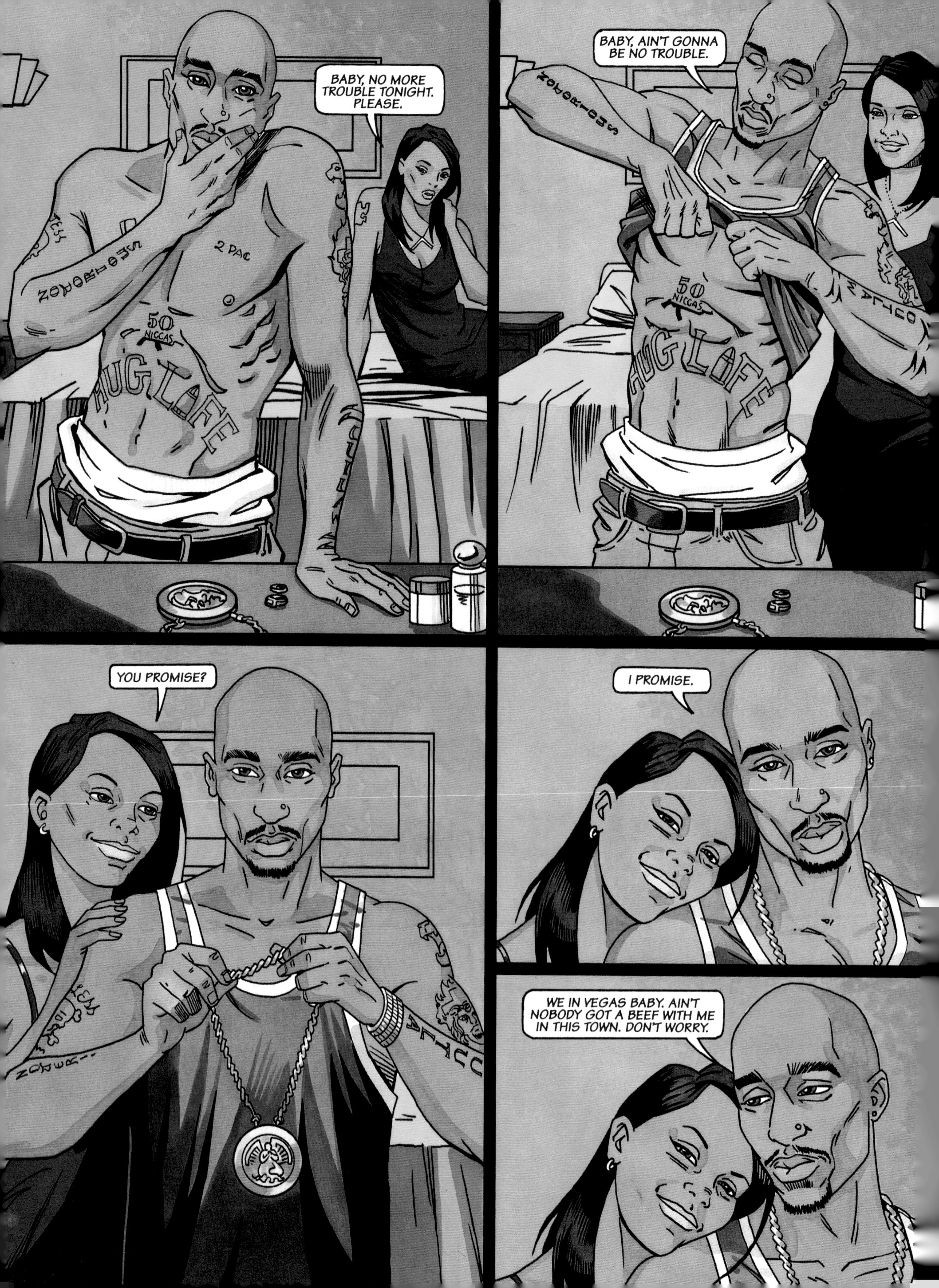
BABY, NO MORE TROUBLE TONIGHT. PLEASE.
BABY, AIN'T GONNA BE NO TROUBLE.
YOU PROMISE?
I PROMISE.
WE IN VEGAS BABY. AIN'T NOBODY GOT A BEEF WITH ME IN THIS TOWN. DON'T WORRY.

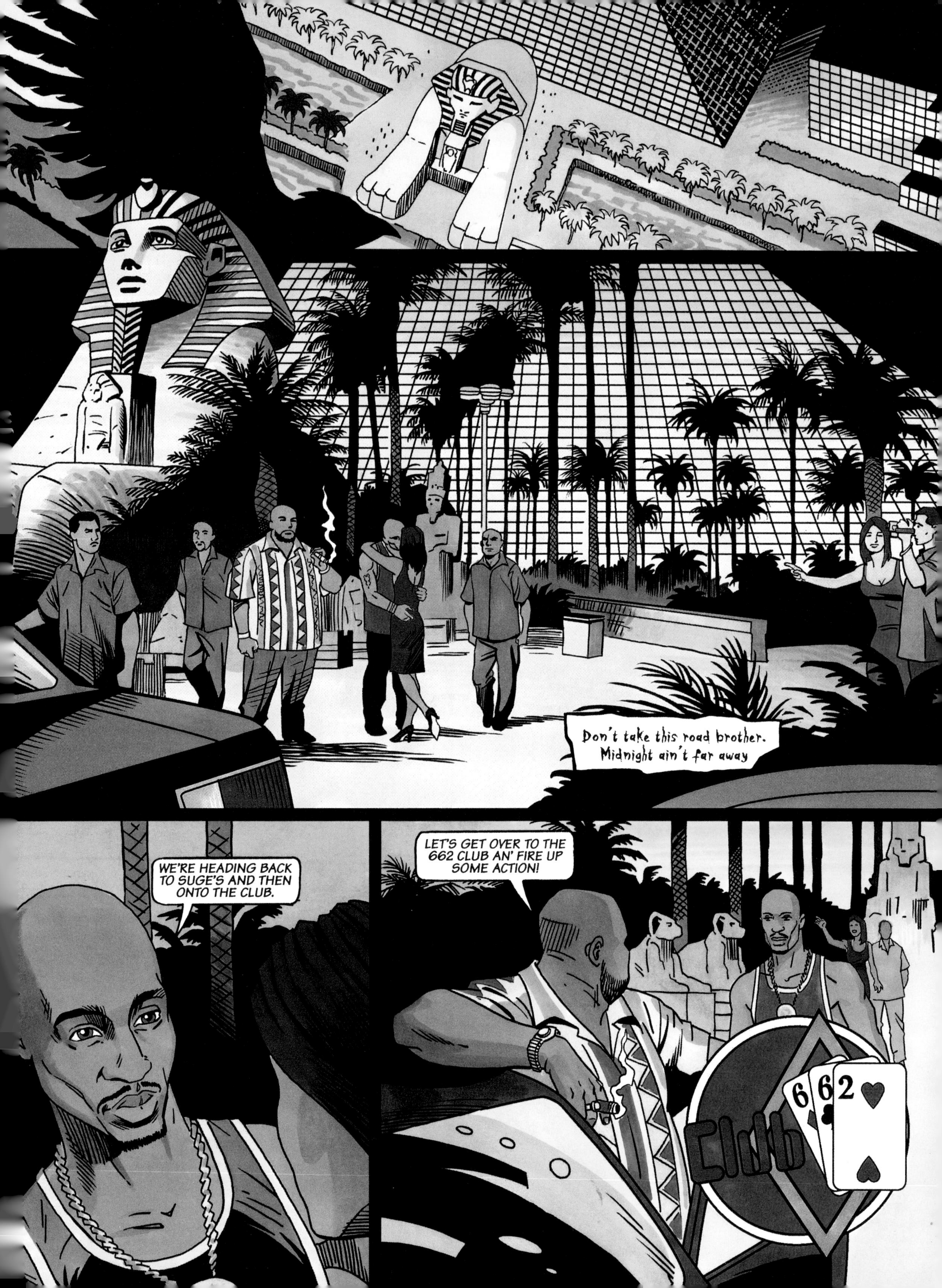
Don't take this road brother. Midnight ain't far away
WE'RE HEADING BACK TO SUGE'S AND THEN ONTO THE CLUB.
LET'S GET OVER TO THE 662 CLUB AN' FIRE UP SOME ACTION!
Club 662

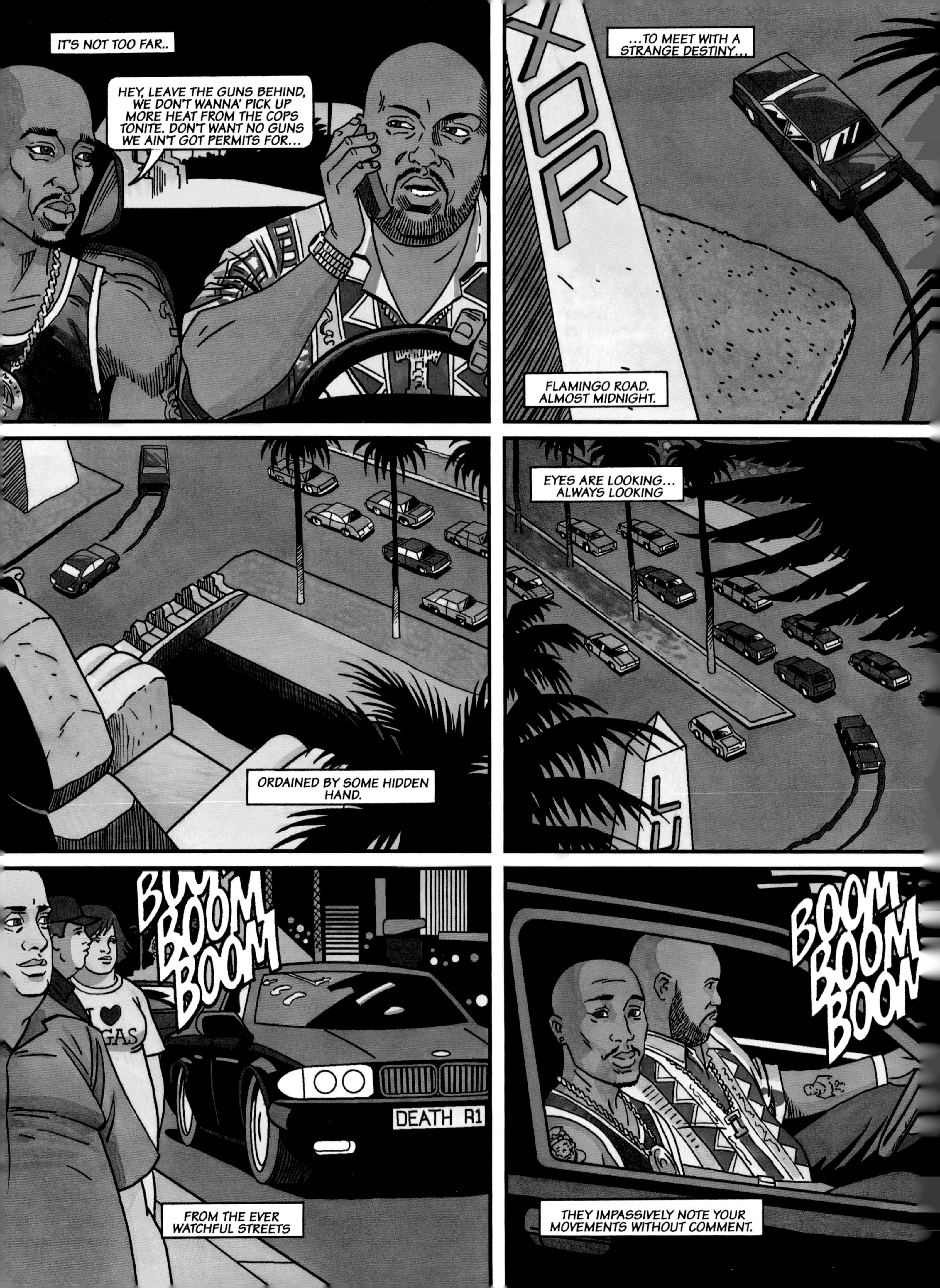
IT'S NOT TOO FAR..
HEY, LEAVE THE GUNS BEHIND, WE DON'T WANNA' PICK UP MORE HEAT FROM THE COPS TONITE. DON'T WANT NO GUNS WE AIN'T GOT PERMITS FOR...
...TO MEET WITH A STRANGE DESTINY...
FLAMINGO ROAD. ALMOST MIDNIGHT.
ORDAINED BY SOME HIDDEN HAND.
EYES ARE LOOKING... ALWAYS LOOKING
BOOM BOOM BOOM
DEATH R1
FROM THE EVER WATCHFUL STREETS
BOOM BOOM BOOM
THEY IMPASSIVELY NOTE YOUR MOVEMENTS WITHOUT COMMENT.

MORE TROUBLE HERE?
OOM OOM OOM OOM
PLEASE SIR, WOULD YOU TURN DOWN YOUR MUSIC?
R JUST A BRIEF PAUSE
OK! I'M GONNA LET YOU GO WITHOUT A TICKET THIS TIME…
Casin
MORE LUCKY ESCAPES?
CAN YOU BELIEVE THAT FUCKING COP? NO TICKET OR NOTHING?
MAYBE HE A FAN.
W MUCH LUCK YOU GOT LEFT? WE ARE NEARER TO 662…
PHOTOS VIDEO
FLAMINGO IS UP HERE… 662 IS RIGHT AROUND THE CORNER.
COOL.
STOP
GO
RED LITE – ANOTHER PAUSE
½ HR PHOTO VIDEO
DEATH R1
Don't take this road brother
SMILES – RECOGNITION.
HEY PAC, WHOOOO, WHEY YOU GUYS GOING?
STOP
THIS ROAD IS A DEAD END

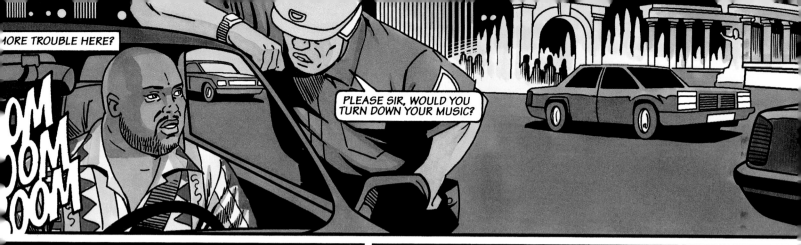

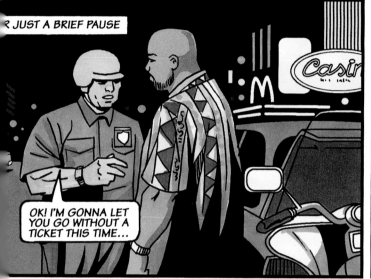

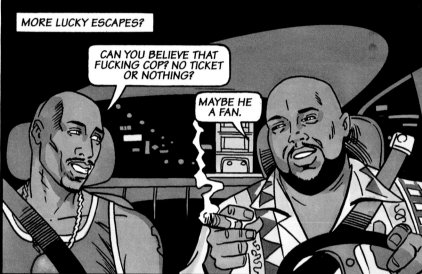

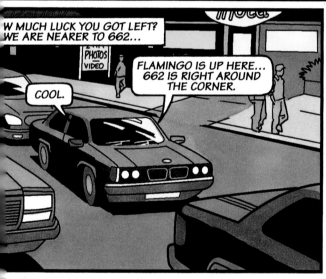

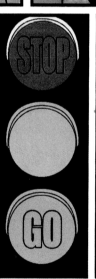

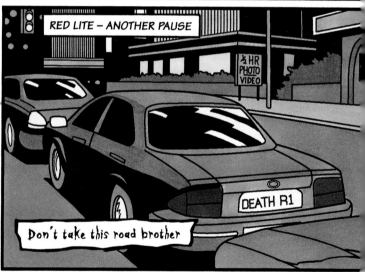

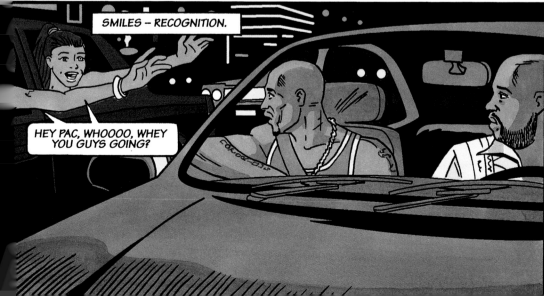

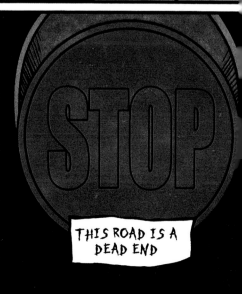

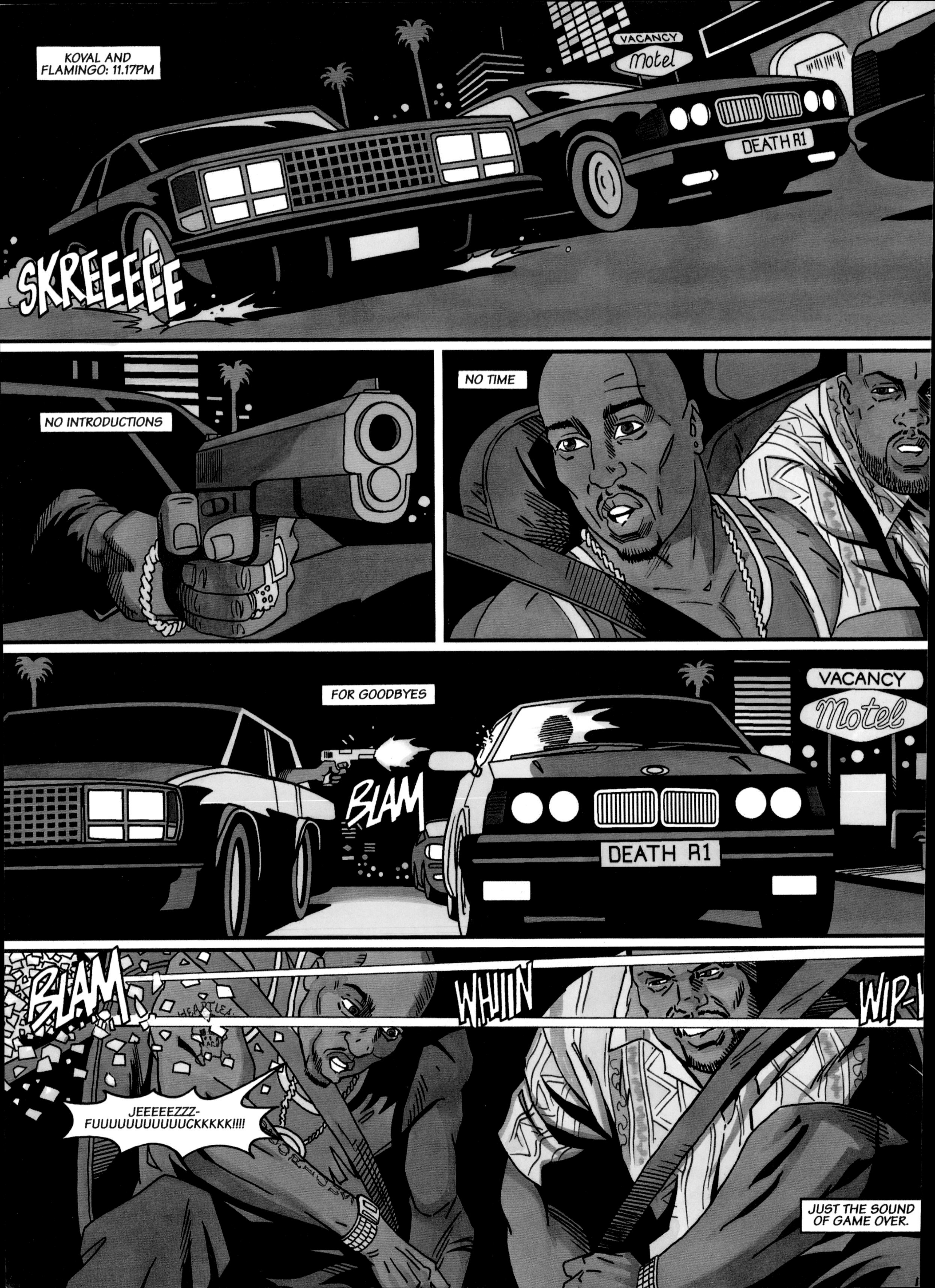

KOVAL AND FLAMINGO: 11.17PM
VACANCY
Motel
DEATH R1
SKREEEEEE
NO INTRODUCTIONS
NO TIME
FOR GOODBYES
VACANCY
Motel
BLAM
DEATH R1
BLAM
WHIIN
WIP-
JEEEEEZZZ-FUUUUUUUUUUUCKKKKK!!!!
JUST THE SOUND OF GAME OVER.

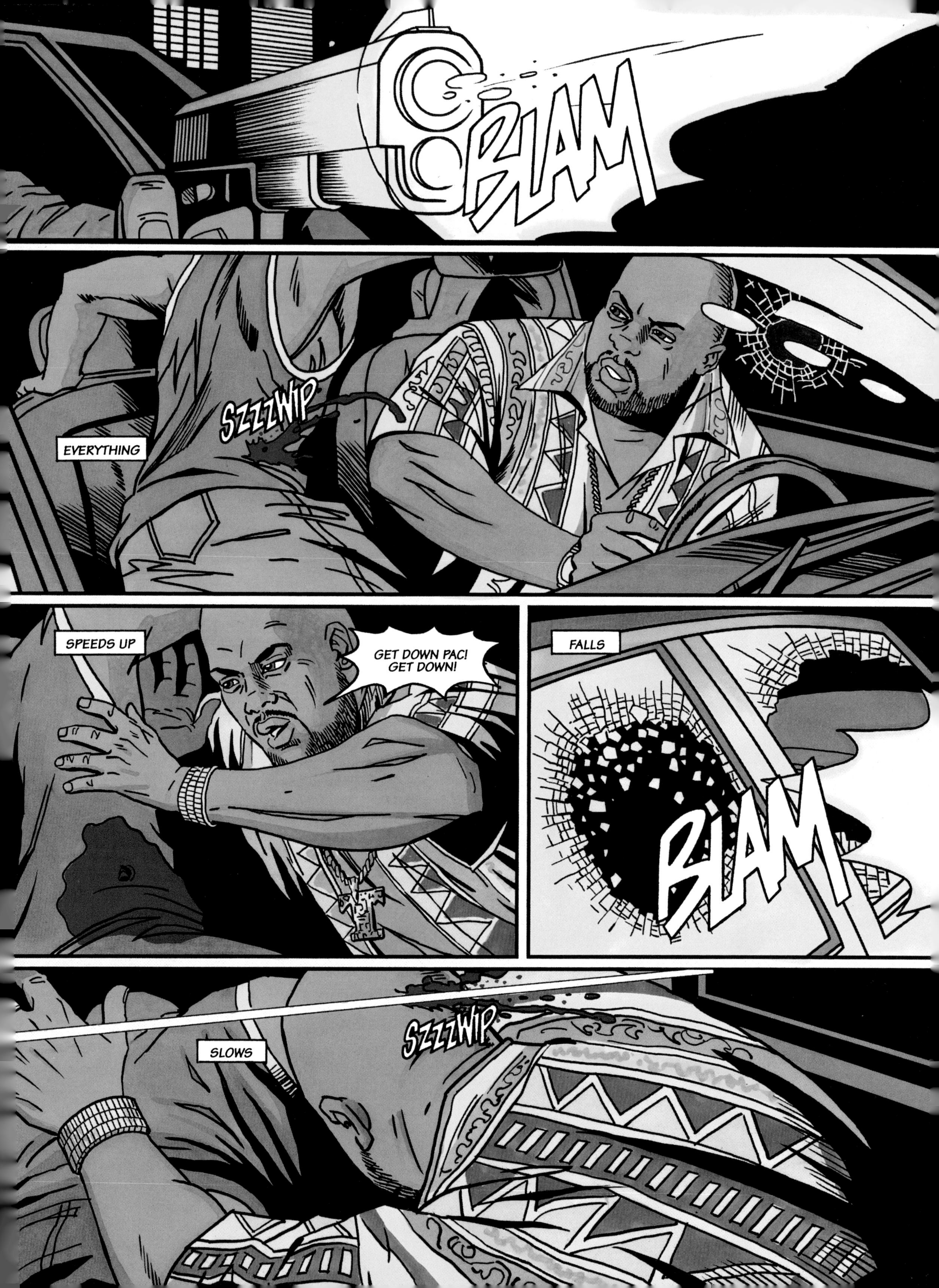
BLAM
EVERYTHING
SZZZWIP
SPEEDS UP
GET DOWN PAC!
GET DOWN!
FALLS
BLAM
SLOWS
SZZZWIP

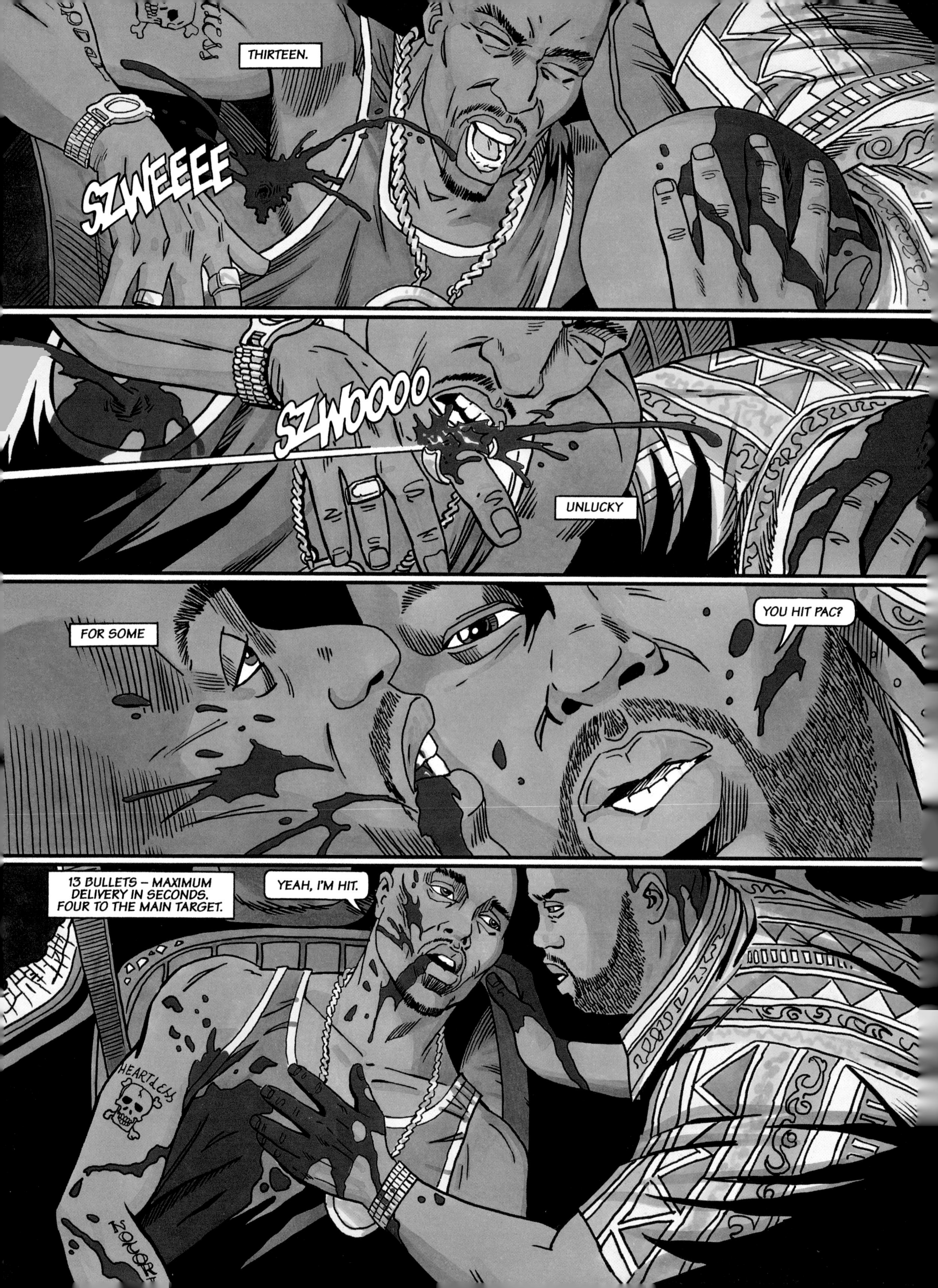

THIRTEEN.
SZWEEEE
SZWOOOO
UNLUCKY
FOR SOME
YOU HIT PAC?
13 BULLETS – MAXIMUM DELIVERY IN SECONDS. FOUR TO THE MAIN TARGET.
YEAH, I'M HIT.
HEARTLESS

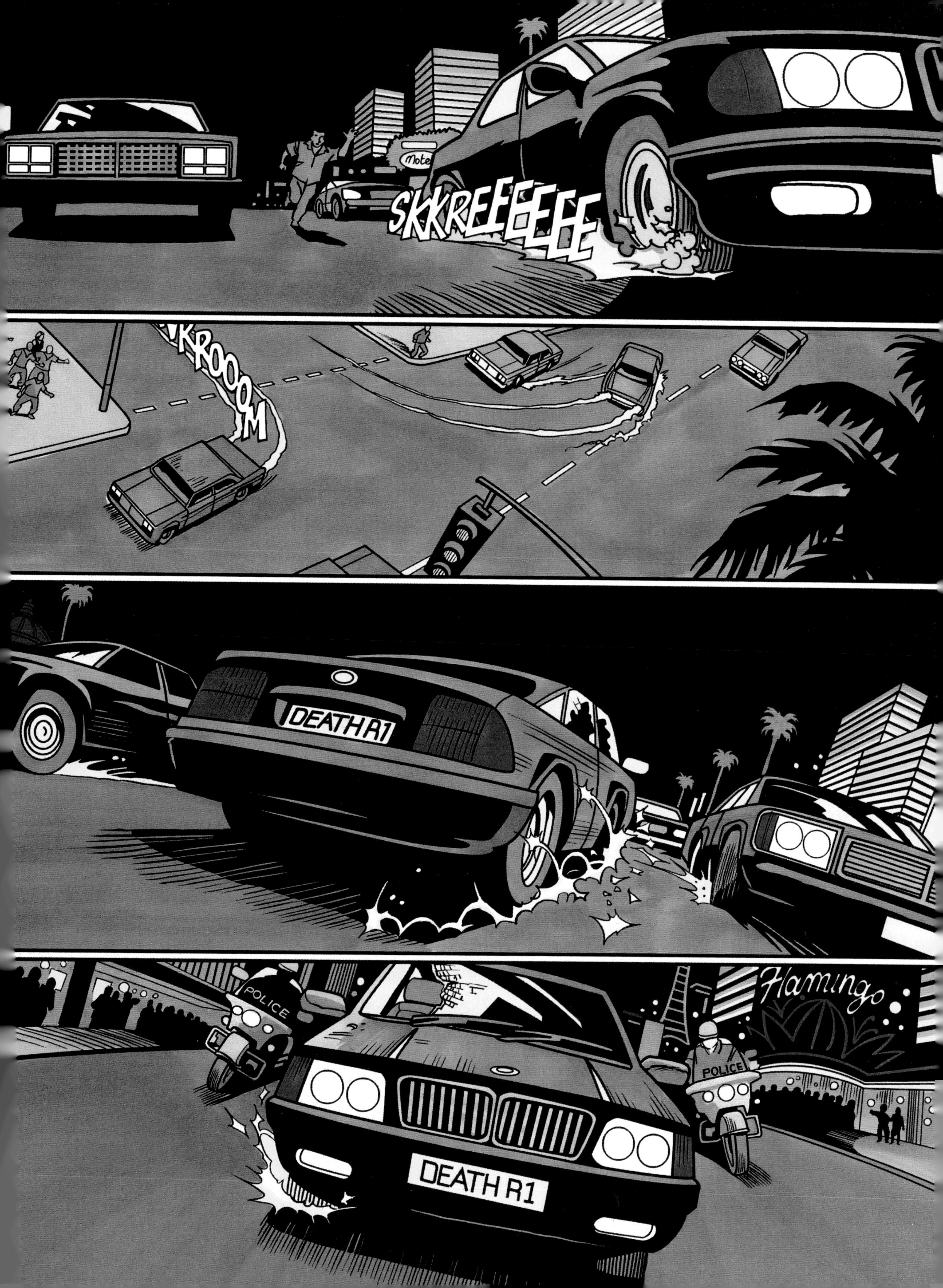

Motel
SKKREEEEEEE
KROOOOM
DEATH R1
POLICE
Flamingo
POLICE
DEATH R1

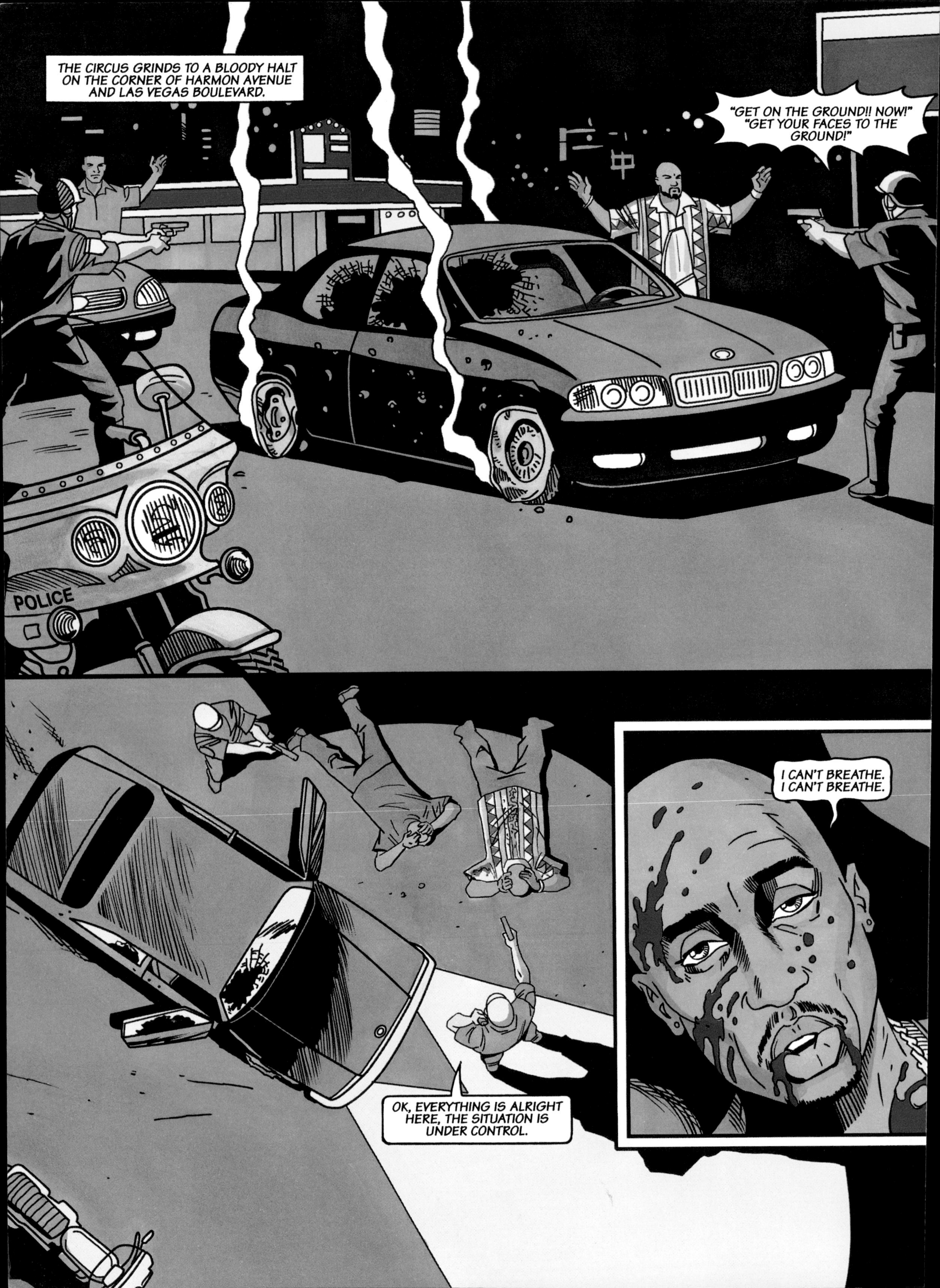
THE CIRCUS GRINDS TO A BLOODY HALT ON THE CORNER OF HARMON AVENUE AND LAS VEGAS BOULEVARD.
"GET ON THE GROUND!! NOW!" "GET YOUR FACES TO THE GROUND!"
POLICE
I CAN'T BREATHE. I CAN'T BREATHE.
OK, EVERYTHING IS ALRIGHT HERE, THE SITUATION IS UNDER CONTROL.

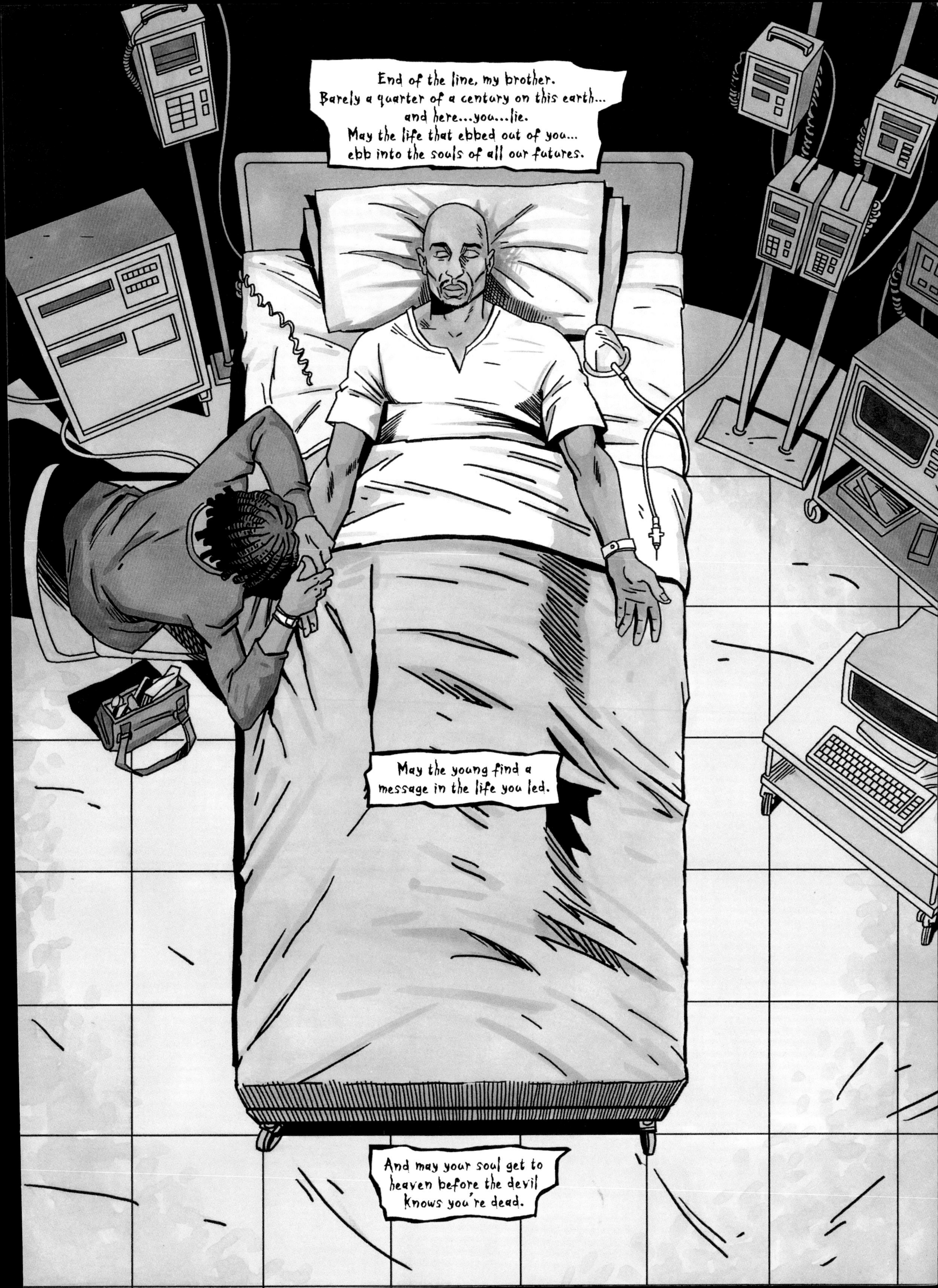
End of the line, my brother. Barely a quarter of a century on this earth... and here...you...lie. May the life that ebbed out of you... ebb into the souls of all our futures.
May the young find a message in the life you led.
And may your soul get to heaven before the devil knows you're dead.

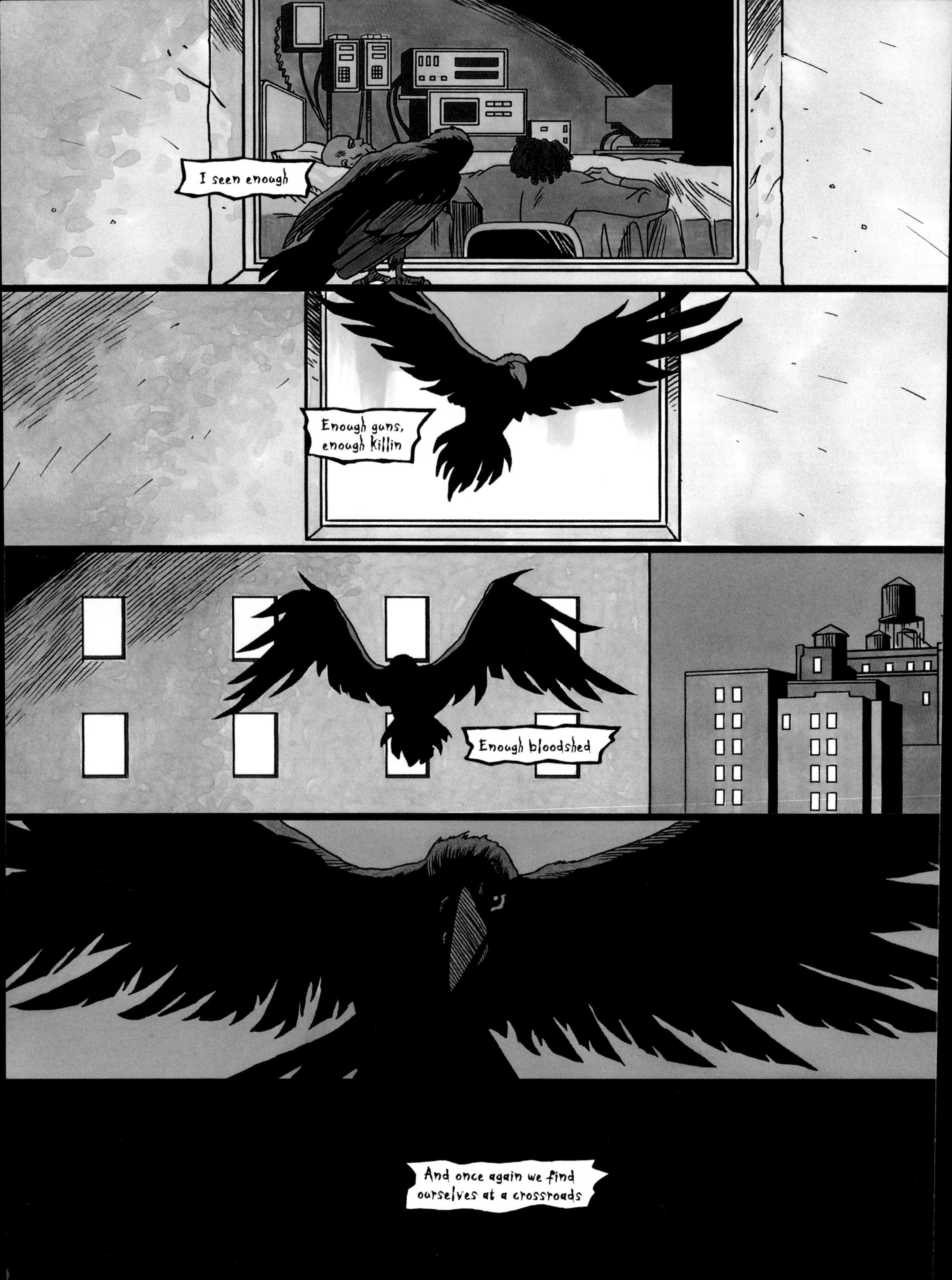
I seen enough
Enough guns, enough killin
Enough bloodshed
And once again we find ourselves at a crossroads

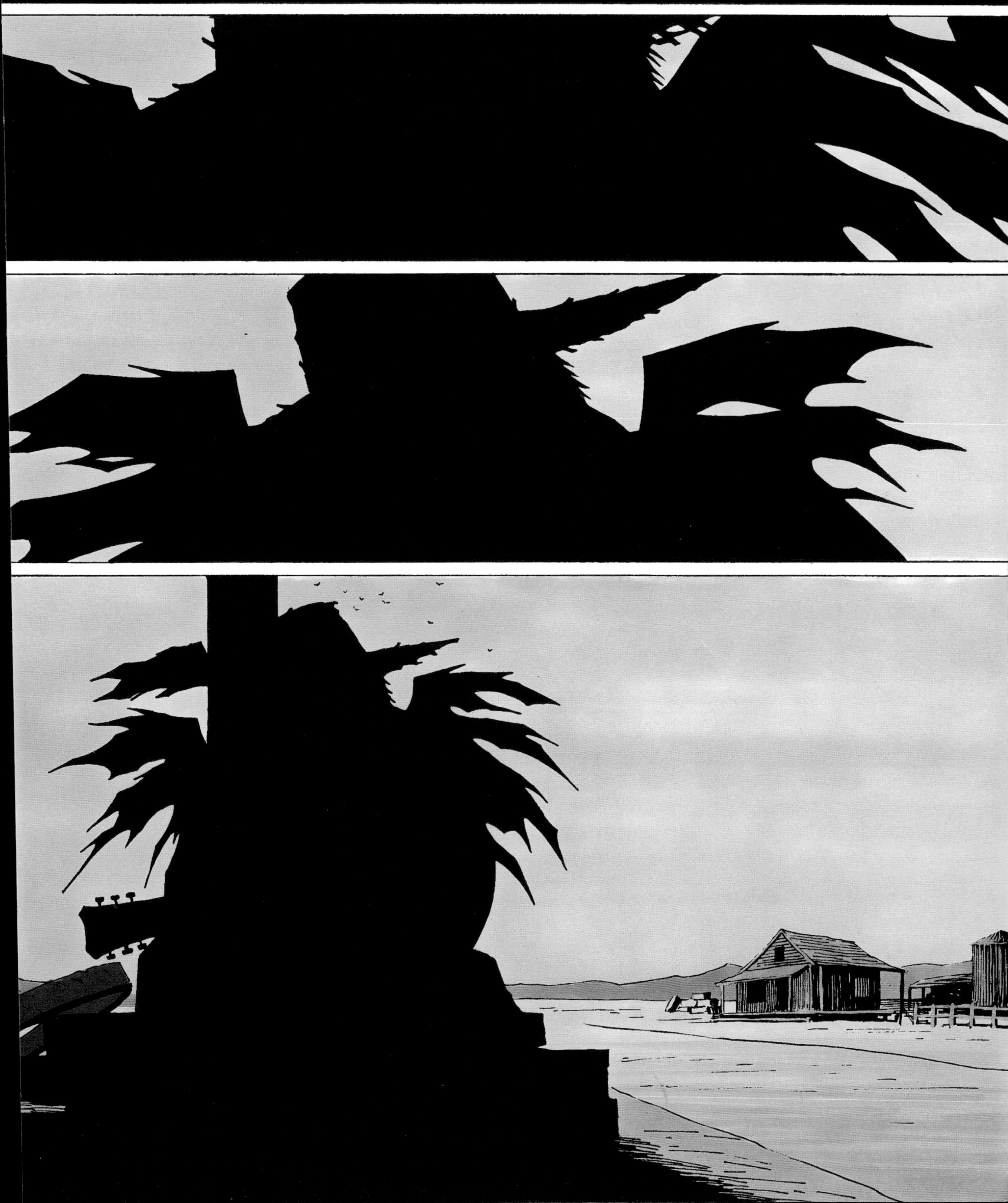

In the United States, the so-called Jim Crow laws (or Black Codes) were made to enforce racial segregation, and included laws that would prevent African-Americans from doing things that a white person could do. For instance, Jim Crow laws regulated separate use of water fountains and separate seating sections on public transport. Jim Crow laws varied between communities and states.

The first Jim Crow law was passed in 1723, when blacks in the state of Virginia were stripped of the right to vote and own property. The later passage of Black Codes, which attempted to return freed slaves to bondage in fact, rather than name, by Southern legislatures immediately after the American Civil War led to the policy of Reconstruction, in which the federal government intervened to protect the rights conferred on black Americans by the 13th, 14th, and 15th Amendments to the Constitution of the United States and the Civil Rights Acts of 1866 and 1875.

Reconstruction ended, however, in 1877. In its aftermath the resurgent white elites, who referred to themselves as redeemers, undid many of the civil rights gains that black Americans had made during Reconstruction, passing laws that mandated discrimination by both local governments and by private citizens. As an example, many state governments prevented blacks from voting by requiring poll taxes and literacy tests, both of which were not enforced on whites due to grandfather clauses. One common "literacy test" was to require the black would-be voter to recite the entire US constitution and Declaration of Independence from memory.

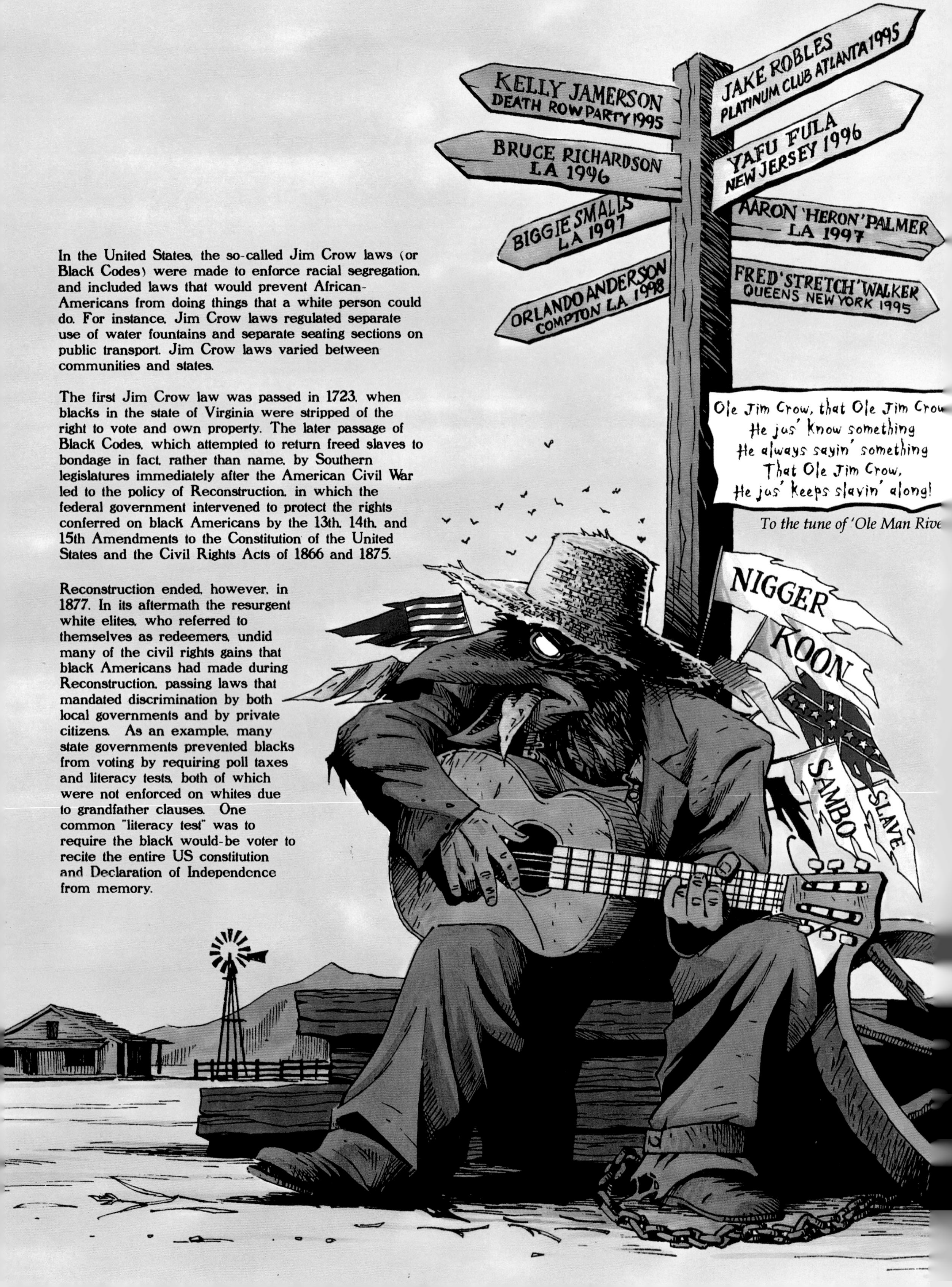
KELLY JAMERSON
DEATH ROW PARTY 1995
JAKE ROBLES
PLATINUM CLUB ATLANTA 1995
BRUCE RICHARDSON
LA 1996
YAFU FULA
NEW JERSEY 1996
BIGGIE SMALLS
LA 1997
AARON 'HERON' PALMER
LA 1997
ORLANDO ANDERSON
COMPTON LA 1998
FRED 'STRETCH' WALKER
QUEENS NEW YORK 1995
Ole Jim Crow, that Ole Jim Crow
He jus' know something
He always sayin' something
That Ole Jim Crow,
He jus' keeps slavin' along!
NIGGER
KOON
SAMBO
SLAVE
To the tune of 'Ole Man River'

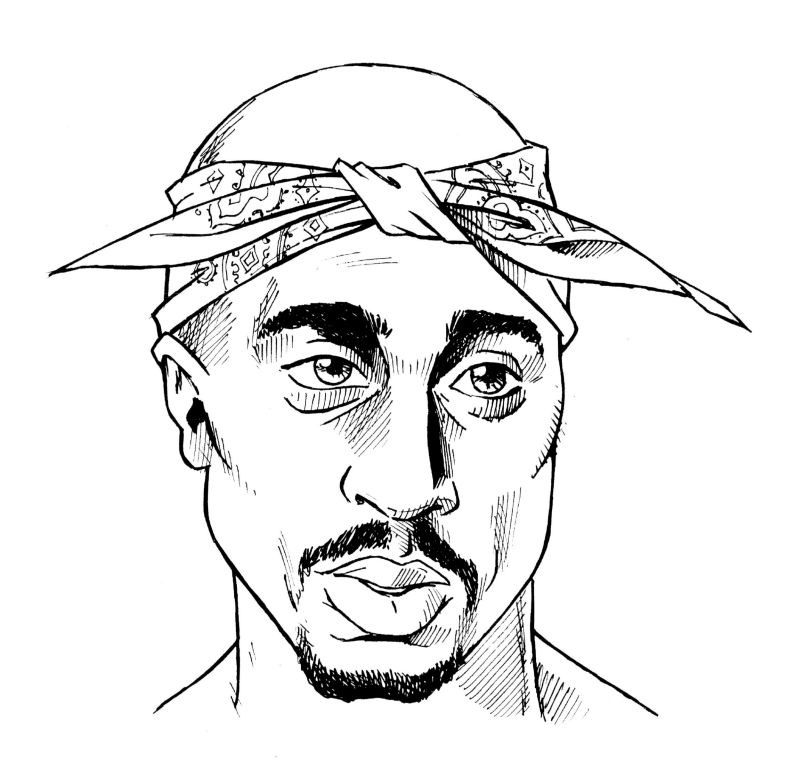

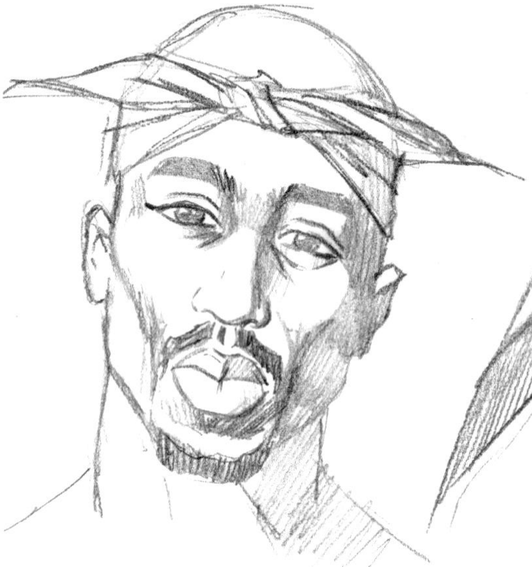

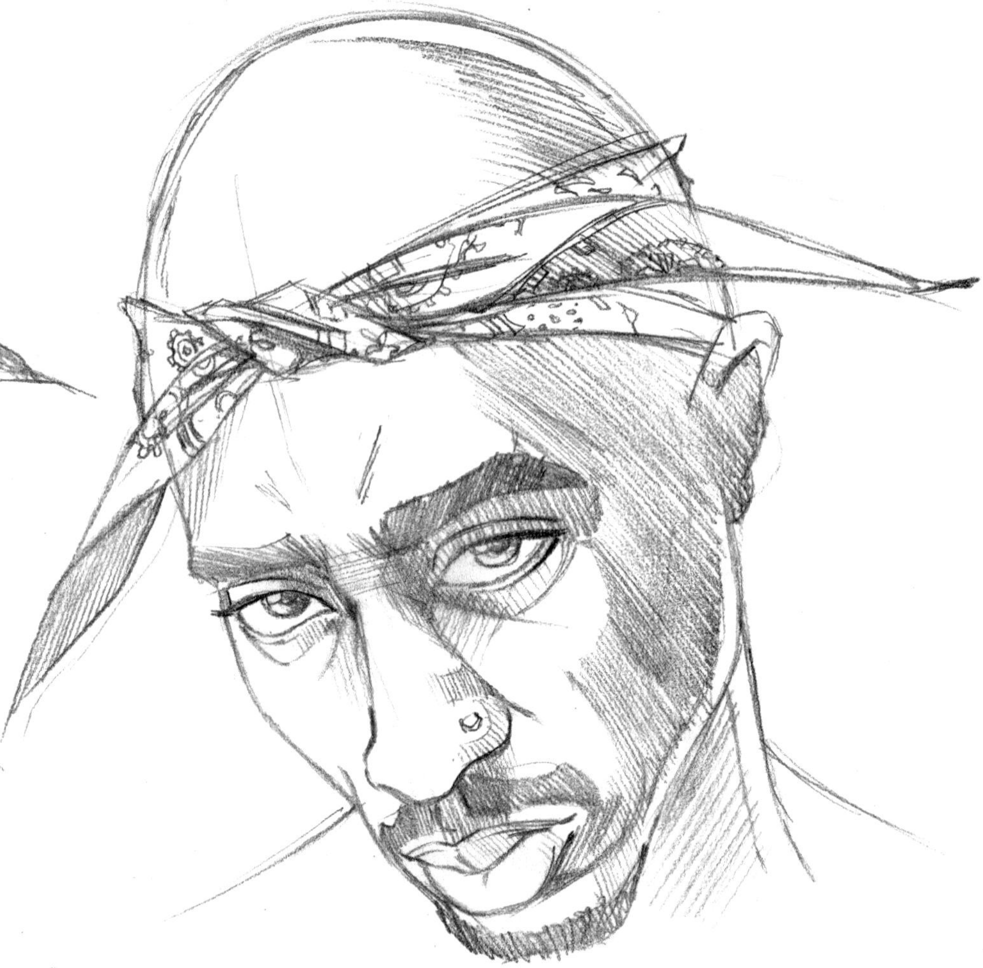

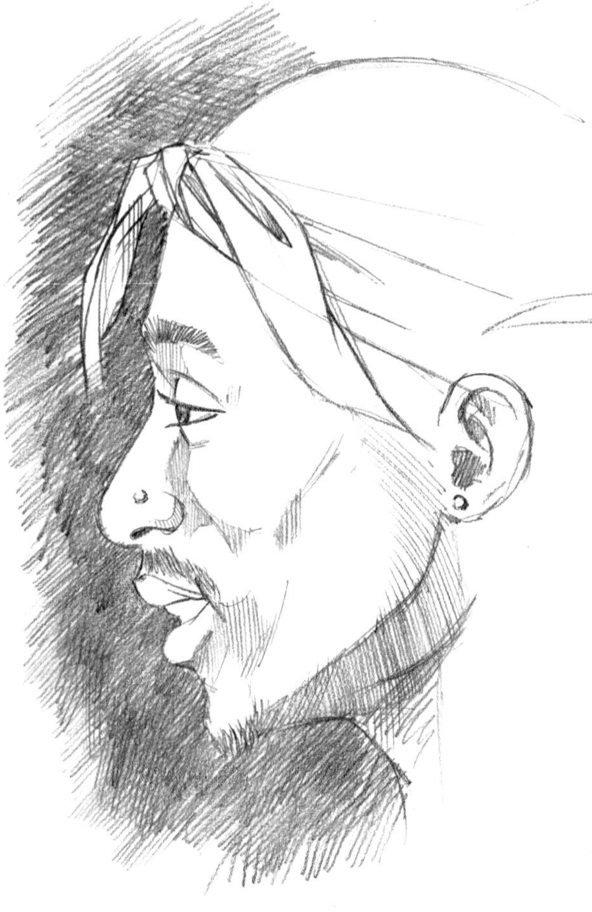

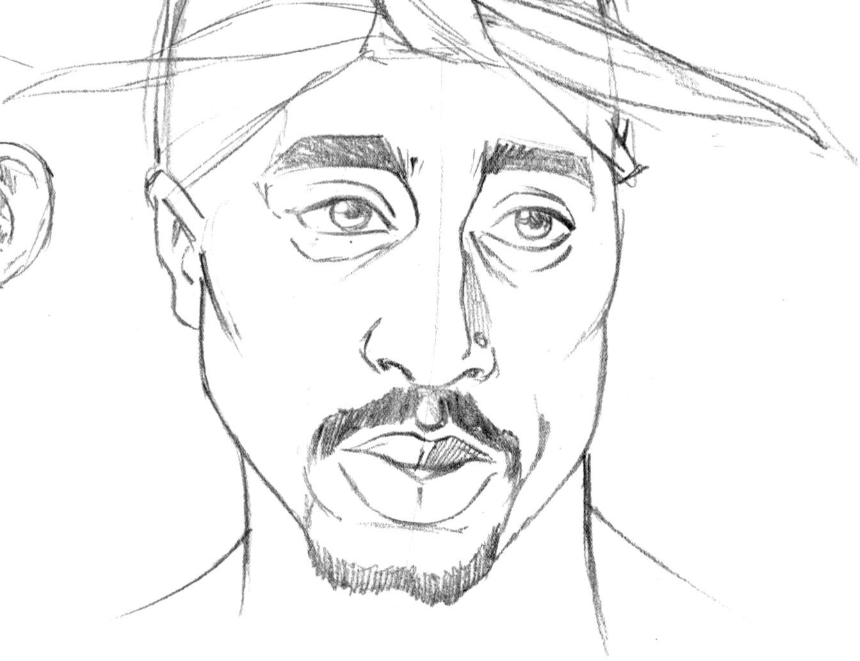